Wicked
Herkimer
County

Wicked Herkimer County

Caryl Hopson and
Susan R. Perkins, *Editors*

Published by The History Press
Charleston, SC
www.historypress.com

Copyright © 2021 by Caryl Hopson and Susan Perkins
All rights reserved

Front cover, top from left to right: Herkimer County Historical Society; Library of Congress; Little Falls Historical Society; Herkimer County Historical Society; *bottom from left to right*: Herkimer County Historical Society; courtesy of Little Falls Historical Society.
Back cover, top left: editors' collection; *top right*: public domain; *center*: Fultonhistory.com; *bottom left*: public domain; *bottom*: courtesy of Herkimer County Historical Society.

First published 2021

Manufactured in the United States

ISBN 9781467148795

Library of Congress Control Number: 2021941044

Notice: The information in this book is true and complete to the best of our knowledge. It is offered without guarantee on the part of the authors or The History Press. The authors and The History Press disclaim all liability in connection with the use of this book.

All rights reserved. No part of this book may be reproduced or transmitted in any form whatsoever without prior written permission from the publisher except in the case of brief quotations embodied in critical articles and reviews.

This book is dedicated to the Friends of Historic Herkimer County for their praiseworthy efforts to save and renovate the 1834 Herkimer County Jail, the "temporary residence" of some fascinating lawbreakers, a few of whose stories are shared in the pages of this book.

CONTENTS

Foreword, by James M. Greiner   9
Acknowledgements   11

1. Grave Behavior   13
2. The Body Snatching of Harry Burrell   17
3. Blond of Thirty Summers   26
4. Oliver Curtis Perry   30
5. No Minor Offense   36
6. The Troubled Life of Alton Vincent   40
7. The Backlash of Infidelity   48
8. The Church Lady and the Forest Ranger   52
9. Fanny, the Female Firebug   56
10. The Houdini of Horse Thieves   59
11. When Yeggs Hit Herkimer County   63
12. The Textile Strike Riot   68
13. The Case of the Rat-Fink Roommate   77
14. Organized Crime in Herkimer County   80
15. Grace under Pressure   84
16. Wild, Wild Beaver River   86
17. He Shot Her in the Corset   91
18. Don't Ask Any Questions   95
19. The Murder of Winifred Getman   99
20. Trial to Triumph: An Immigrant Family's Story   102

Contents

21. The Gillette Cell	109
22. Criminal Melodrama	119
23. Shootout at Camp Utica in Old Forge	128
24. Recollections of a Wicked Boy in Herkimer	132
25. Bones in a Burnt Barn	137
26. Burglary and Fire in East Schuyler	144
27. Killer Ghosts	147
Notes	153
Bibliography	157
About Friends of Historic Herkimer County	169
About the Editors	171

FOREWORD

In the summer of 1923, Theodore Dreiser stood at the Historic Four Corners in Herkimer, New York. This was the final leg of his tour of places associated with the subject of his next book. Having read the voluminous trial transcript of *The People vs. Chester Gillette*, Dreiser wanted to see the courtroom where the trial took place and the jail that held the accused before making the trip to Utica and then to the scene of the crime, Big Moose Lake.

The Herkimer County Court House hadn't changed since the 1906 trial of Chester Gillette. When Dreiser walked into the courtroom, he gazed upward to an ornate tin ceiling that stretched the entire width of the building. The horseshoe-shaped gallery where reporters and townspeople sat to view the trial looked down upon the rows of benches and the jury box. Across the street it was the same. The cell that housed Gillette was just the same as it had been in 1906.

Two years later, Dreiser published *An American Tragedy*, lighting a fire of interest in a murder case that to this day hasn't been put out. Each year, researchers, murder buffs and tourists from all over the country descend upon the Four Corners. They visit the Herkimer County Historical Society, which has files of newspaper clippings, the trial transcripts and the handcuffs worn by Chester while he was being escorted from the jail to the courthouse and back again. Their next stop is the Herkimer County Court House, which, they soon discover, has changed over the years. The gallery was taken down and the immense courtroom reconfigured to accommodate offices in the

Foreword

1930s, when the county received a Works Progress Administration (WPA) grant. The beautiful tin ceiling was hidden by tiles during the energy crisis in the 1970s. The jury box is gone, and so is the judge's bench. The only thing that remains is the few dozen wooden benches.

What isn't a disappointment is the cell Chester occupied in the 1834 Herkimer County Jail. The only thing that has changed is the plumbing in the two-person cell. As you will discover in this book, the cell was a temporary home to numerous felons until 1976, when a new jail was constructed.

If Theodore Dreiser ever needed material for a new book, all he had to do was pay Herkimer County another visit. He would have had plenty of material to work with. He would have uncovered a wide range of colorful characters, murderous doings and scandalous behavior. Dreiser never came back here, but fortunately for you, the reader, a few people have come forward to do research and write about *Wicked Herkimer County*.

—James M. Greiner
Herkimer County historian
Friends of Historic Herkimer County, president

ACKNOWLEDGEMENTS

We were excited for another opportunity to write about the "wild side" of Herkimer County's history and to bring back many of the contributing authors from *Murder & Mayhem in Herkimer County* to join several new contributors for this publication. They each conducted extensive research to bring out the story in their own writing style, and we thank them for their work and ready participation in sharing these stories in *Wicked Herkimer County*. Our featured contributing authors are Diane Fagan Affleck, Shayla Clark, Barbara Dunadee, James Greiner, Angela Harris, Caryl and James Hopson, Deborah Huxtable Kidder, David Krutz, Gregg Lawrence, Patrick Luppino, Peg Masters, Susan Perkins, "Det Smada," Jeffrey Steele, Patricia Masi Stock, David Waite, Roberta Walsh and Dennis Webster.

Pictures really help bring out the imagery of a story. We greatly appreciate the assistance we received from Mary Haefele, Rob Royce, Donna Loomis Rubin, the Village of Herkimer and village trustee Maria Vennara Fiorentino, the Herkimer County Historical Society, Little Falls Historical Society, Mike Disotelle at the History Room at Ilion Free Public Library, Paula Everett of Mount Greenwood Cemetery (Chicago, Illinois) and Upstate Medical University (Syracuse) for sharing images with us.

In many cases, a photograph or image, especially an older one, has a blemish or two that needs correction. We are lucky to have the help of Darryl Grubner, our "photograph guru." Darryl can do wonders with fixing these images, and we thank him for his helping hand with the images in our book.

Finally, we thank the Friends of Historic Herkimer County for sponsoring our publication, making it possible to bring these stories to you today.

1
GRAVE BEHAVIOR

by Jeffrey Steele

Many would likely feel that disinterring the recently dead in the middle of the night in order to spirit the body away with the intention of dissecting it is a wicked act. However, some medical students in the nineteenth century thought of such an action as something they simply had to do in the name of science. These two differing viewpoints were not just part of some theoretical debate in Herkimer County in the early 1800s.

Operating from 1812 to 1841, near the intersection of Hardscrabble Road and Route 29 in the town of Fairfield, was the College of Physicians and Surgeons of the Western District of New York, better known by its common name, the Fairfield Medical College. The study of medicine in the nineteenth century was still working its way toward modern science, and if one wanted to learn how to become a doctor or a surgeon, one had to gain firsthand experience with the inner workings of the human body. The goal was to do this in a scholarly and legal manner, but occasionally, Fairfield's medical students took things into their own hands—literally—by raiding the graveyards of nearby communities, much to the anger and disgust of neighboring residents. Many of these gruesome and, believe it or not, occasionally humorous tales about wickedly extracurricular nighttime excursions by Fairfield's students have come down through the years, some possibly closer to the truth than others.

Illustration of Fairfield Medical College by R.H. Pease (undated). *Courtesy of Archives & Special Collections, Upstate Medical University.*

One of the first major, and often retold, stories reportedly occurred in 1817. A young and popular schoolteacher in the town of Norway, Miss Saloma Whiting, died after a short illness. Soon after her burial in the White Creek cemetery, visitors to her grave noticed that it had been disturbed and her body removed. Suspicion immediately fell on the nearby medical college, and a mob, reportedly with firearms and even a cannon, quickly formed and prepared to march to Fairfield. The students of Fairfield initially tried to deny they had Whiting's body. But after being threatened with armed outrage, they quickly decided to compromise by admitting they had the body and returned it to avoid any assault on their campus. Reportedly, after Whiting was reinterred, armed volunteers continued to guard her grave nightly until any further threat to it passed.

Grave robbing was certainly not part of Fairfield's approved curriculum. After the Whiting incident, and possibly others, the college's trustees and professors certainly tried to make that clear. In January 1819, the trustees approved a resolution that stated, "If any student in any way attached to the said College shall hereafter…be concerned in digging up or in removing any dead human body to be used as an anatomical subject…he shall be forthwith dismissed from the College and his name given up to some proper authority for public prosecution." The State of New York, in 1820, tried to help Fairfield acquire bodies for scientific dissection in a more acceptable manner by allowing the medical college to legally acquire the bodies of inmates who died in Auburn State Prison unless those bodies were taken away first by the deceased's friends or relatives. These measures likely helped mitigate the problem of students raiding nearby graves, but stories of incidents continued.

In 1826, Samuel Perry of the town of Newport murdered his wife with a knife and then tried to commit suicide by stabbing himself, only to survive. He was charged with first-degree murder. A jury found him guilty, and the judge sentenced him to hang. During an appeals process, in which Perry was arguing insanity, jailors discovered him in his cell after he had slit his own throat. Authorities returned his body for burial, and there were rumors that some of Fairfield's students might have wanted it, so a watch was kept over his grave for a number of nights. On the fourth night after burial, two "tramps" reportedly approached the guards and offered them strong whiskey. After the guards awoke and sobered up much later, they discovered that both the tramps and Perry's body had disappeared. Apparently, there was no wide outrage over the theft of the body of a murderer who had killed himself, as there had been during the Whiting incident, and the matter quietly passed.

An 1833 letter written by a Fairfield student to a cousin who had graduated from Fairfield the year before tells that there were more incidents that year in which citizens in nearby Little Falls and Middleville became quite upset following attempts to disinter bodies in their communities. There is also an oft-repeated, though undated, story of an occasion when a mob of outraged citizens descended on the campus after hearing rumors of grave robberies. As the story goes, the students heard advance notice of the impending mob and quickly placed fourteen bodies that they had under a trapdoor in the floor of their laboratory, which they then covered. They then placed old bones and dried specimens of dissected muscles all around the laboratory, which were common enough to see at a medical school, so that when the mob arrived, it appeared there were no bodies and nothing was amiss, even after a thorough search. The mob soon departed, thinking all the rumors must have been false. Over the years, nearby residents continued to worry about their loved ones' bodies being stolen and used for medical dissection. An elderly resident recollecting the past recorded that he had an uncle in the town of Norway who had his wife's grave placed near his bedroom window and then surrounded by a high fence to make sure nothing happened to it. This same resident also told of a grave he knew at Little Falls that was protected by brick and mortar for the same reason.

There is one more oft-repeated, although also undated, story from the nearby area of Prospect that is too good not to share. A student from Fairfield was attempting to bring a body back to the college by propping it upright in a horse and buggy, trying to disguise it as if it was a passenger. When the horse and buggy stopped at a tavern and the student got out, a pair of pranksters noticed how odd things looked and investigated. After discovering that the rather stiff, upright passenger still in the buggy was actually a corpse wrapped in a blanket, they decided to teach the student a lesson. One of the pranksters substituted himself in the blanket and stayed perfectly still when the student returned to the buggy and drove off. Some distance down the road, at a quiet and lonely spot, the prankster poked the driver in the side and supposedly asked for a drink. As the tale goes, the driver hasn't been seen since. I guess it goes to show that wicked tricks can also be played on those who are acting wickedly themselves.

2

THE BODY SNATCHING OF HARRY BURRELL

by David Krutz

Monday night, April 22, 1879, was moonless and dark. At about 9:30 p.m., two figures dressed in black slipped through a broken gate on the Church Street side of the Village Burying Grounds in Little Falls. The two men, William Van Alstyne and Thomas "Happy Jack" Kane, trod the walking path between the gravestones to the receiving vault in the cemetery's northwest end. All was quiet except for the faint sounds of laughter and music wafting up the hill from a birthday party on Monroe Street.

At the vault, "Happy Jack" took a seat on the stoop while the strongly built Van Alstyne wrested the padlock off of the vault's door with a crowbar he had stolen from Shipman's barn. Inside the vault, the pair was confronted by a second door. This time, the padlock would not give, so the two ghouls used the crowbar and muscle power to force an opening in the door just large enough for them to enter singly. A set of steps brought them down into the blackness of the vault and to the smells of mold, embalming fluid, decay and death.

"Happy Jack" lit a candle with their single match and discarded the candle's paper wrapper onto the vault's floor, an otherwise simple act that would lead to the grave robbers' arrest. The candle's dim halo of light illuminated more than a dozen wooden boxes arranged on shelves. Inside those boxes lay caskets containing the grim reaper's winter harvest— bodies of the departed who had died when the ground was frozen too hard to inter them. One wooden box lay on the floor, so that was the one they chose to open first.

The top of the box was screwed shut, but fortunately for the thieves, a workman had left a screwdriver in the vault, and the box was quickly opened. Upon opening the casket, Van Alstyne and Kane stared down at the pinched and ashen face of poor little twelve-year-old Isabel Murphy. She had died four months earlier. The casket was closed, and the top of the wooden box was put on loosely. Isabel Murphy was not the body they were seeking. The next box they chose did contain the body they sought.

The box was dragged from a shelf, and its cover was removed, revealing a plate on the casket that read "Harry Burrell." Here was their man. Inside the silk-lined casket lay the body of one of the richest and most prominent men Little Falls had ever known. Harry Burrell had died five weeks earlier and was awaiting burial in the village of his youth, Salisbury. After ascertaining that the corpse was truly that of Burrell, Van Alstyne and Kane closed the casket lid, snuffed out the candle and exited the vault. Van Alstyne remarked to Kane that the "stiff" still smelled quite "fresh."

The fiends left the cemetery the way they had entered, walked down Church Street to Ann Street, proceeded down Ann and separated on Mill Street. It was now about 10:30 p.m. Van Alstyne went to McGuirk's saloon to get more matches and have a drink or two, while Kane went to Thomas Fox's blacksmith shop. As planned, Van Alstyne met "Happy Jack" at Fox's and with the crowbar made short work of the lock on the blacksmith's barn. Once inside, a horse was harnessed to Fox's wagon, an old horse blanket was thrown into the wagon bed and the pair left to collect their body. Instead of taking the direct route to the cemetery, the wagon was driven east on the River Road, up into Manheim and entered Little Falls on Monroe Street.

Reaching the cemetery around midnight, Van Alstyne and Kane tied the horse to a fence and made their way back to the vault. All was as they had left it. To prepare the corpse for travel, Harry Burrell's tie was removed to bind his wrists together, and a "lowering" strap bound his ankles. Ever the thief, Van Alstyne could not resist pocketing Burrell's silver collar buttons. The body was then wrapped in the old horse blanket, dragged from the vault and loaded onto the wagon. On the way out of the vault, Burrell's head caught on the inside metal door, and a part of his scalp and hair were torn off and left clinging to the door. Harry Burrell's slippers were left in the coffin.

The wagon was driven back down Monroe Street and on into Manheim, where River Road was taken back toward Little Falls. Instead of reentering

Burrell family plot at Church Street Cemetery in Little Falls. *Editors' collection*.

the village, Van Alstyne crossed Finck's bridge and drove the wagon westward up the steep incline of Fall Hill and on to Jacksonburg. It was his intent to confuse anyone attempting to track the route that the body was taken.

In Jacksonburg, the wagon was halted at the old Jacksonburg hotel near the canal lock. The structure had been converted into a barn and

Headstone of Harry Burrell. *Editors' collection.*

two apartments. (Jacksonburg was a small hamlet located about midway between Little Falls and Mohawk on present-day Route 5S. At one time, it had a general store, a hotel and a post office.) There, Van Alstyne and Kane were met by Nathan "Pop" Lewis, who resided in one of the "barn" apartments. ("Pop" Lewis gained his nickname because he operated a small "soda pop" manufacturing and bottling operation.) Lewis wrapped one of his blankets around the corpse, and the trio carried Burrell's body to the barn, where it was stowed underneath the barn in a crawl space. With daylight coming on, Van Alstyne drove hard back over Fall Hill and Finck's bridge to Fox's shop, where they returned the thoroughly exhausted horse and the wagon without incident. Both men then walked home and went to bed.

Harry Burrell, William Van Alstyne and Thomas Kane

Harry Burrell was born in Massachusetts in 1797. When he was seven years old, his family moved to Salisbury. At an early age, he began working in the cheese-making industry. A bright youth, Harry developed innovative ideas for improved cheese making, equipment and the marketing of cheese. He

Harry Burrell (1797–1879).
Courtesy of Little Falls Historical Society.

owned dairy farms in and around Salisbury and eventually moved to Little Falls in 1850. Harry became a butter and cheese buyer, representing interests in New York City and foreign markets, and he was known as the father of the renowned Little Falls cheese market. He accumulated a fortune and, through his enterprise and public spirit, was a beloved Little Falls citizen. After his death in March 1879, at the age of eighty-one, his son David H. Burrell took over the family business.

William Van Alstyne (aka William Keating, William King and William Catin) was born in Oneida, New York. He was twenty-two years old in 1879. An orphan at the tender age of five, he was raised by an uncle. Although a very intelligent boy, early on, William turned to "evil ways"; his relatives predicted that he would spend the bulk of his life in prison. In 1875, he absconded with funds from the "soda pop" company where he worked in Oneida. He made his rounds collecting money from the company's customers, pocketed the cash and hopped a train out of town. For the next few years, he rambled around the country, eventually settling down in Little Falls in October 1878. William was described as tall, well built, clean shaven and quite handsome.

Thomas Kane was twenty-three years old in 1879. He resided in Little Falls all of his life. Illiterate and "slow witted," as his nineteenth-century nickname "Happy Jack" suggests, he earned a living as a hack driver, an Erie Canal deckhand and a thief. Kane was classed with the "thieves, idlers and desperadoes" who inhabited the village's south side.

Outrage and Clues

On Tuesday morning, April 23, 1879, just hours after the body snatching, workmen intending to inter a casket discovered the desecration of the vault and the taking of Harry Burrell's body. The Little Falls police were contacted, as was David Burrell. News of the heinous crime spread like wildfire throughout the village, and a crowd formed in the cemetery. Police officer Charles Shepardson entered the vault and discovered what would be two key pieces of evidence. He found that the thieves had used a candle (noted by wax drippings) and discovered the torn paper (part of a handbill) that had been discarded on the vault's floor.

About the same time as this was occurring, Thomas Fox noticed that his horse and wagon had been "borrowed" the night before—the horse was "lathered up" after a hard workout—and a blanket had been stolen. The theft of Fox's horse and wagon was quickly connected to the grave robbery. The wagon had a wobbly rear wheel, which left distinctive marks, as did one of the horse's shoes, such tracks being found near the cemetery. Police also recovered from the wagon bed a button (later found to be from Van Alstyne's coat) and a hank of scalp and hair similar to what was found on the vault's inner door.

Outrage over the crime was such in Little Falls that a citizens' patrol, numbering over thirty men, was quickly formed. Every entryway into the village was guarded, as were both ends of Finck's bridge. All wagonloads were examined, and every stranger was stopped and questioned. Other citizens inspected possible hiding places in Little Falls or fanned out into the countryside. David Burrell immediately hired two detectives, one of whom, Wheeler from Utica, was famous throughout the Mohawk Valley for his investigative work. The *Utica Herald* sent a full-time correspondent to cover the story. In short, Van Alstyne and Kane had disturbed a hornet's nest.

Napoleon Casler, who owned a grocery store on Ann Street, now stepped forward to provide the key clue that brought the grave robbers to heel. Hearing about how a candle was used in the robbery, Casler told an interesting story. On the afternoon of the robbery, Kane had entered his store and purchased only one item, a candle, for two cents. Casler tore a handbill lying on his counter and wrapped the candle in it. Casler had kept the other part of the handbill, and when Officer Shepardson produced the piece found on the vault's floor, it matched perfectly Casler's piece. The Little Falls police now knew that Thomas Kane had been in the cemetery vault that night and promptly arrested him.

Discovery of the Body and Arrests

Wednesday, April 24, effectively brought the case to its end. On that morning, Rodney House, who lived in a residence close by the barn in Jacksonburg, went looking for one of his chickens that liked to roost under the barn. Instead of finding his chicken, he found the body of Harry Burrell. Rodney ran to get his brother Squire, and the two House men, along with Nathan Lewis, rode into Little Falls to tell David Burrell of their finding. Squire House was a well-respected, model citizen, but on the way to Little Falls, greed got a hold of him. On reaching the offices of David Burrell, Squire informed David that he had a clue as to where Harry's body might be found, but it would cost $1,000 (about $25,000 in 2020 terms) for him to divulge it. When David refused to pay such a reward, Squire dropped his request to $500, but that, too, was refused. Finally, House fessed up and said that they had found the body and would take David Burrell to it.

Arriving at the Jacksonburg barn, David Burrell was one of the first men to crawl through the hay and manure beneath the barn to retrieve his father's body. On the way back to Little Falls, David sat in the box of the wagon, cradling the corpse. (Three days later, a second funeral was conducted for Harry Burrell. His body was interred in a specially designed grave in the Little Falls Village Cemetery. Some say that a concrete slab was placed over the coffin.)

The Little Falls police took special interest in the two blankets covering the corpse. One of the blankets was identified as that which was stolen from Fox's shop, while the other was found to have been owned by Nathan Lewis. This evidence, along with the fact that Lewis occupied the apartment directly above where the body was found, led to the issuance of a warrant for the arrest of "Pop" Lewis. Police found a quite drunk Lewis in a Little Falls saloon, arrested him and sent him to the Herkimer jail alongside Happy Jack Kane. William Van Alstyne was soon to join his co-conspirators.

On Friday night preceding the grave robbery, William Van Alstyne had broken down the front door of the home of Alvin Richmond on West John Street in Little Falls. Waving a pistol in Richmond's face, Van Alstyne delivered the classic robber's request, "Your money or your life." But Alvin Richmond resisted, and when Richmond's wife screamed "Murder!" out of their bedroom window, Van Alstyne made a hasty retreat. Van Alstyne was arrested and, like his cohorts, was sent to the Herkimer jailhouse.

Confessions and Judgments

Detective Wheeler of Utica stepped in at this point. A few years earlier, Wheeler had gained the confidence of Thomas Kane, getting Happy Jack to deliver state's evidence against his accomplices in a railway theft case. Wheeler, knowing that Kane trusted him, convinced Kane to confess to the body snatching. Kane's confession implicated Van Alstyne and Nathan Lewis as the other principals in the theft. Confronted with Kane's confession, Pop Lewis also confessed. Lewis's confession disclosed that the body snatching was not a spur-of-the-moment crime but had been planned for over a month and involved many other individuals.

Lewis confessed that Van Alstyne had proposed the stealing of Harry Burrell's body back in March, just a few days after his death. Van Alstyne thought that the Burrell family would pay $20,000 (about $500,000 in 2020) to get their father back. Over the next few weeks, John "Body" McGuirk, Adam Bellinger, Nathan Lewis, Van Alstyne and he had planned the caper, including dry runs, inspection of the vault, locating a horse and wagon to use and determining potential hiding places for the body. Thomas Kane had been a late addition to the plot. Based on Lewis's admissions, McGuirk, Bellinger and Wright Lewis were arrested as accessories to the crime.

Trials and sentencings took place the last week of April and the first week of May 1879. John McGuirk and Nathan Lewis were sentenced to five years hard labor, Adam Bellinger and Wright Lewis received ten years (both men had long prior criminal records) and Thomas Kane got three years. William Van Alstyne, the mastermind of the grave robbery and the perpetrator of the

Alvin Richmond home invasion, was sentenced to ten years in prison for the Richmond crime and five years for the body snatching. All of the prisoners were soon hauled off to either the Auburn or Onondaga penitentiaries. Squire House was arrested in October and charged with his attempt to extort money from David Burrell.

Thanks to the efforts of Police Chief Smith, Officers Shepardson and Collins, Detective Wheeler, David H. Burrell and many other citizens of Little Falls, less than one week transpired between the theft of Harry Burrell's body, its recovery and the apprehension of those responsible. And within a month, justice had been served on the miscreants.

As a side note, the barn where the corpse was found was disassembled a few years after the event. It was transported from Jacksonburg to "Pigeon Hill" in Little Falls, where it was converted into a house.

3
BLOND OF THIRTY SUMMERS

by James and Caryl Hopson

Malinda Humphrey, by all accounts, was a dazzler. Her blond, flowing hair enchanted two men in Little Falls. One man, her husband, Thomas Humphrey, fathered three children with Malinda, while another man whisked her away to the Midwest with her children in tow.

A sensation was caused in the village of Little Falls in October 1879, when, according to the local newspaper the *Evening Times*, a "blonde of thirty summers," Malinda (née Quackenbush) Humphrey, stole not only their children but also $600 of her husband's money to be with her true love, one David Halloway.

But let's start at the beginning. Malinda's husband, Thomas Humphrey, was a veteran of the Civil War, a member of the 118th Regiment, Pennsylvania Infantry. He was wounded twice, at Petersburg, Virginia, and at Peeble's Farm in 1864, and he served at Gettysburg. After the war, he ventured north to Little Falls, seeking employment. He found it at the Little Falls Knitting Mill on Elizabeth Street near the Mohawk River. It was there that fate took a hand, as he met the lovely Malinda, who was then in her late teens and only half his age. Love evidently ensued, and they were married. Over the course of the next ten years, three children were born to the couple, first Charles in 1869, then Elizabeth (Lizzie) about 1873 and Edward about 1877. The marriage by all accounts was a happy one until the unhappy year of 1879, when David Halloway, the "fascinating Englishman," according to

Where it all began: Little Falls Knitting Mill. *Courtesy of Little Falls Historical Society.*

the *Evening Times*, stepped into the picture. David had acquired a job at the knitting mill and developed a friendship, a very close friendship, with young Malinda, who by that time was also working at the factory. This was the setting for scandal: two men and one young woman employed and working closely together.

Husband Thomas, by then fifty-two years old, was suffering an ailment to the eyes that caused him to be nearly blind. But he was also blind, according to the gossip at the knitting mill, to the relationship between his young wife and David Halloway. Thomas had recently received a $1,300 pension for his service in the Civil War. The government payment came at just the right time to pay for a trip to a New York City doctor to be treated for his blindness. And while Thomas was away, Malinda and David schemed to get away, too. In their plans, Malinda stole about half of the pension money from Thomas. She told her cuckolded husband she would use the money to put a down payment on a house. No such payment was ever made.

Instead, Malinda sweet-talked Thomas into withdrawing $600 from the Herkimer County National Bank, where she then exchanged it for a certificate of deposit in her own name. She and David used that money to hop a train bound for Utica and points west, taking the three children with them. David was hardly guiltless, for it was a love quadrangle. He left behind a wife with a parting gift of $20 for her troubles. Malinda's father,

Abram Quackenbush, found out about the illicit getaway and chased after them to Utica, but the train had already left. He returned to Little Falls and, inexplicably, while husband Thomas was still away, had all of the household belongings packed away for future use. Thomas would come back to a house not only empty of his wife and children but also of the furnishings therein.

A heartbroken Thomas endeavored to find the children, but according to a later account in the *Albany Argus* in 1889, he was unsuccessful. Without wife or family, he spent his final years at the National Home for Disabled Volunteer Soldiers in Dayton, Ohio.

The story does not end here. Thomas and Malinda's daughter, Lizzie, just six at the time she was taken away, remembered her father and grandparents, Abram and Mary Quackenbush. She made it a priority in her life to find them. She believed her father to be dead and was searching for her grandmother, who she remembered to be in Little Falls. She wrote to the local postmaster, who forwarded the letter to Charles Bailey, owner of the Little Falls Knitting Mill. Bailey took a keen interest in the letter and the entire story. He took it upon himself to track down Thomas, whom he knew to reside at the soldiers' home in Dayton. Bailey brought about a reunion through his efforts when it was revealed to Lizzie that her father was indeed alive. Father and daughter began exchanging letters. We can only hope that the reconciliation was a joyful one.

The affair between Malinda and David that started in 1879 kept this runaway couple together for their remaining years. Malinda listed herself

Left: Headstone of Malinda Helliwell (1850–1915) at Mount Greenwood Cemetery in Chicago, Illinois. She is buried next to David. *Courtesy of Paula Everett, Mount Greenwood Cemetery*.

Right: Headstone of David Helliwell (1838–1902). Note the spelling difference from "Halloway," as reported in the local paper in 1879. *Courtesy of Paula Everett, Mount Greenwood Cemetery*.

The Dayton Soldiers' Monument at Dayton National Cemetery. Thomas's grave is in Section I, Row 9, Site 46 near the monument. *Credit: National Park Service, Photo by Ted, CC BY-SA 2.0, https://commons.wikimedia.org/w/index.php?curid=21636526.*

as a wife to David, even though no evidence of a formal divorce was ever found. They were buried together in their final destination, Chicago, Illinois, at Mount Greenwood Cemetery, where their graves have them identified by David's last name, which is written as Helliwell.

Thomas Humphrey received a farewell befitting a soldier for his country when he died in 1895. He is buried at the Dayton National Cemetery near the Dayton Soldiers' Monument. We'd like to believe his final years were peaceful in finding the whereabouts of his children and overcoming the wicked ways of an unfaithful wife of "thirty summer years."

4
OLIVER CURTIS PERRY

by Deborah Huxtable Kidder

"I realize that society will not tolerate men of the stamp I proved myself. I realize that when a man once steps outside the law every hand is raised against him and he is hunted down like a wild beast. I do not know anything about socialism or anarchism, but I know that when a man takes it upon himself to equalize unjustly distributed wealth by robbing express trains he makes a mistake," noted our villain in the *Troy Daily Times* of April 1895. Certainly, along his way, as both a youth and an adult, hands were raised against him. Oliver Curtis Perry was vilified in the press, chased by local law enforcement, wanted by federal agents and abused by jailers.

Perry enters the national stage in 1891. In the 1800s, both Wells Fargo and the American Express Company were transporting monies and other valuables on specially designated express railroad cars. At a time when express cars were shown to be vulnerable to attack in the Wild West and train robberies had been sensationalized by the American press, it isn't surprising that a robbery in Herkimer County would make news across New York State and throughout the nation.

Oliver Curtis Perry, as one might expect of a man who turns to crime, had a troubled youth. Born in September 1865 or 1866, his birth and early years were spent in the "Irish Settlement," a now lost community close to Middle Sprite Creek near Lasselsville and Oppenheim in Fulton County, New York. His time there was short-lived; before he was ten years old, his mother left her husband and Oliver. When his father remarried, the new wife did not want the young son in her family home. Although the grandmother took care of him briefly, it is reported that he was placed either in an orphanage or on a farm for youthful offenders. As a drifter, he lived by whatever means he could, not necessarily within the limits of the law. His style of living caught up with him in Rochester, where he was arrested for stealing a suit of clothes. As a juvenile, he was sentenced to the Western House of Refuge, the first state-managed reformatory in the United States, housing males under the age of eighteen who had been convicted in courts. Oliver Curtis Perry must have found this near-prison atmosphere a very difficult adjustment from his roving ways. He attempted escape and certainly reacted adversely to the conditions there. In a report by his keepers from 1883, he obtained false keys, stole weapons and knives from the shop and had a "low and vile disposition" (Spargo, p. 110). They petitioned to have him moved to an adult prison, and he was sent to the Monroe County penitentiary.

Mugshot of Oliver Curtis Perry. *Library of Congress.*

According to records and newspaper reports, from 1885, when he left Monroe County, until 1890, he traveled out west, spent some time in the Stillwater prison in Minnesota and worked as a ranch hand, a cowboy and in the South as an overseer. Back in Troy, New York, it appears he tried to reform his wicked ways by attending the prayer meetings of a Miss Amelia Haskell, joined a Presbyterian church and worked a number of odd jobs. It might be assumed that the job he had with a railroad as a brakeman on the express train helped his later endeavors.

Oliver Curtis Perry was not able to keep to the straight and narrow path. The lure of easy money was too great. The exploits of the famous train robbers such as Jesse James and his gang in the West may have given him encouragement to try his hand. Later sensationalized accounts have him romantically involved with a farmer's daughter out west with whom he wanted to settle down and so needed a nest egg for a home. His life until that point certainly leads one to surmise he would never have been able to settle for the simple life of a day-job worker. For whatever reasons, Oliver Curtis Perry began to make plans.

The American Express Special, number 31, was known to leave Albany daily. No passenger cars were on the Express, just company cars loaded with goods and a "money car," the last of the train. Perry was prepared on the night of September 29, 1891, as two weeks before, he had sequestered a gun, a saw, a jackknife and a gimlet, as well as a small drill hand tool. Reports do not state how he got on the Express near Frankfort, New York. Once onboard, Perry proceeded to use the gimlet and the saw on the lower panel of the door to the money car. With enough holes, the weakened panel gave way, and with the aid of a box, he levered his way into the car through the hole. Bert Moore, the armed security guard—termed the "messenger" in railroad vernacular—was located in the middle section of the three-partitioned car. When Perry entered that section, the agent jumped up but was easily overtaken by surprise. Perry picked up Moore's revolver, gave a warning shot and held the agent at gunpoint. The masked intruder made Moore open the safe, and the thief took several sacks that he put into a larger shoulder bag. Perry then climbed backward through the hole and cut the coupling that regulated the brakes on the train. As the American Express Special slowed, Perry jumped from the train and fled into the night with the loot. Oliver Curtis Perry had made the first single-handed train robbery!

In his tale of the deed, Perry recounts that his pants were torn and his hat jammed, and he was shaken and flustered. So he determined not to try to catch the next train returning to Troy. He roamed around the countryside near Frankfort. It is not known how Perry left the area. Railroad men, police and Pinkerton agents were hunting the man. It was only on day five, near Alphonso Borden's grove, that two local men found the remains of sacks and envelopes with labels of the American Express. A study of early maps does not show a marker for Borden's grove, but the name of a landowner, J. Borden, can be found near Harbor, which is in an area just west of the village of Frankfort. This spot is close to the Mohawk River, the railroad and a crossing of highways. A variety of press releases in the late 1890s tell of merrymaking at Borden's grove near Harbor. Trips sponsored by such groups as the Elks and the Woman's Christian Temperance Union were made by packet boat on the canal or by rail to the grove for picnics.

An intrepid reporter for the *Utica Daily Press* did his best to find the trail taken by the thief. His report goes into some detail about the surrounding countryside and how easy, from the location where the empty stash was found, it would be to spot any law enforcement making a search. The reporter interviewed a farmer, Erving Vance, who told of a stranger who wandered onto his property. The farmer recalled that the stranger feigned drunkenness, asked directions for a nearby landowner and then wandered off in the opposite direction. Was this Perry or just another vagabond? The description by Vance matched that given by Bert Moore, and the hunt was on for a man of slight build, with a small, dark mustache and standing five feet, nine inches tall.

How much money had Perry been able to steal? Reports vary depending upon the source. The American Express Company, perhaps in an effort to lessen the impact, gave a report of only $1,000, but the empty sacks indicate some jewelry boxes and envelopes tagged at $5,000 worth. An Albany banker remarked that the cars carried nearly $100,000. Whatever the amount, the reporting by the Utica papers brought the crime to the attention of all New York.

Luckily or unluckily for Perry, a railroad crewman who had caught sight of the robber remembered Perry as a fellow train employee. The Pinkerton agents now knew their man. They released a description of Perry that not only covered the essentials, such as height and hair color, but also gave an impressionistic view: "Wrinkles between his eyes give a troubled and thoughtful expression.…He is gentlemanly, polite and effeminate in manner, but acts nervous and uneasy" (*Elmira Telegram*, 1892). His single-handed caper and the feat of stealing from the great American Express brought notoriety to Perry. Although the search was widespread, the man was not to be found. Pinkerton agents at one point were in a room above Perry while he hid in the cellar below. Bert Moore was under pressure as an accomplice, but Perry boldly sent a letter postmarked Ontario absolving Moore of the crime. Even that location evidence did not lead to a capture.

Perry had made off with a haul but by winter had possibly run out of money. And that first robbery may have emboldened him to try again. On February 20, just six months after his initial train theft, he again attempted to rob the American Express, this time as it left Syracuse. The details of this effort have a well-dressed Perry leaping aboard the train, running along the roof line as the train sped west and using a rope and a hook to swing down to the money car to enter it by breaking a glass-fronted door. The express messenger, Daniel McInerney, heard the breaking glass and took up arms. The robber and the messenger exchanged gunfire. McInerney missed; the robber was more successful and damaged the agent's hand. Perry, having donned the same red hood as he had used previously, climbed into the railcar. As McInerney tried to pull the air whistle, Perry shot again, resulting in a grazing of McInerney's head and a thigh wound for the poor train man. By this time, others had been alerted. Perry was having no luck getting

McInerney to open the safe. Perry decided to leave the train as it slowed reaching the next station.

Perry guessed that the train crew would expect him to board a freight car leaving the station, but Perry, now in another disguise, stepped back aboard the Express. He rode it to nearby Lyons and left the train as it slowed approaching the station. An astute trainman, who had seen the robber on the Express, recognized Perry and shouted a warning. The chase was on! Perry commandeered another locomotive and was chased by the Express train going backward in its pursuit. As the Express neared him, Perry reversed his iron horse but had no time to restock the coal. As it slowed, Perry deserted the engine and fled across the fields. Fifty armed men joined in the pursuit. Perry stole horses and cutters and ran for protection near a stone fence but was at last surrounded and, although armed, gave himself up.

Oliver Curtis Perry's exploits made headlines again. He was brought to trial in Wayne County in May. Although there was a chance the trial would be in Herkimer County, where his first theft had taken place, a March 1, 1892 editorial in the *Herkimer Citizen* hoped this would not be so. "Herkimer County does not want this desperado confined here or tried here either.… Wayne County can take just as good care of him as our enterprising sheriff." Perry was convicted on an assortment of charges relating to the robbery in Herkimer and the attempt in Wayne County. His sentence was forty-nine years, and he was hauled off to the Auburn State Prison.

Was that the end of the saga of Oliver Curtis Perry? Not by any means. Perry was not about to give up his freedom. He attempted to escape while still in the county jail and made a daring outbreak from Auburn by finding a hole in a wall and exiting through his neighbor's cell onto the grounds. He was caught before he could leave the prison yard and was beaten by guards. His fight with a fellow prisoner and an attempt to stab a prison guard, as well as the escape, had him spending many sessions in the prison dungeon, once for forty-four days. For these escapades and his increased aggressiveness, he was transferred to the Matteawan Asylum for the Criminally Insane. Perry was not done. In 1885, he and four others were able to escape by means of a metal spoon fashioned into a key. They then went through the attic onto the roof. All were later caught, Perry in New Jersey. By now, Perry had lost any time for good behavior, was given a longer term and had indeed fallen into desperate straits. He had lost weight. A wanted poster photo notation states: "The likeness is a good one but flatters. The face is not so full and the lips are thinner" (*Cortland Contrarian*, 2018). He was sent back to Auburn for a time, where he contrived to blind himself by the use of a board and two saddle needles. Transported to Matteawan, he was able to complete his task of becoming fully blind by rubbing broken glass under his eyelid. In 1901, he was transferred to the newly opened Dannemora Prison. Perry went on hunger strikes, refused to wear clothes and claimed he was being poisoned. Another last try at escape was to build a ladder made of paper to reach a window at the top of his cell. With the help of others, he sent letters to the press about unfair treatment and hoped to achieve a pardon as a blind man not able to further commit crimes. Perry had all the signs of a despairing man confined to prison.

Perry died at Dannemora on September 5, 1930. Throughout his storied adult life and long after his death, Oliver Curtis Perry was able to draw the attention of the press and others. Prison reformers tried to intervene on his behalf. Perry's own written entreaties for better treatment were sometimes allowed past the authorities, and visitors on official tours were able to talk to Perry. Interviews with authorities at the prison were reported as late as 1913, and folks continued to recall Perry's exploits to the papers as human interest pieces. Two songs have been written about this noted train robber. A handful of the verses by the Magic City Trio suffice as a fitting ending to the tale of Oliver Curtis Perry.

> *Oliver Curtis Perry was an outlaw onto himself*
> *He went to rob a train one night with nobody's help*
> *He put on a scarlet hood and wore an iron vest*
> *He carried a pistol and an Indian charm to aid him in his quest…*
> *The Pinkertons and Railroad men finally tracked him down*
> *They put him in the prison close to Dannemora town*
> *He could not escape that jail despite many tries*
> *Protesting his conditions there he drove nails into his eyes*
> *He remained in prison, he never was released*
> *Till all the men who put him there, were forgotten or deceased*
> *They treated him so badly, they were so unkind*
> *They only broke his body, not his spirit nor his mind.*

5

NO MINOR OFFENSE

BY GREGG LAWRENCE

"Partly responsible for the condition of her daughter." In May 1893, those words were the beginning of a process of uncovering an underworld of immorality in the village of Dolgeville, described as a sort of Mafia, an organization of men to destroy young virtue. The old women were left alone, and crimes were committed with the little girls, mere children. It was this that stirred the legislature to action to make a law limiting the age of consent.

Ethel Barger, under the pretense of running a dressmaking shop in the Faville building in Dolgeville, opened a house for the corruption of young girls. Two prostitutes—one as young as fourteen years of age—by the names of Bertha Valentine and Nellie Van Ever went missing after becoming infatuated with some of the attachés of the Cole & Lockwood Circus. When the circus left town for Little Falls, the girls followed. The mother of the Valentine girl swore out an arrest warrant on her daughter and was quoted in the *Utica Observer* accusing the Dolgeville chief of police, James W. Cramer, of knowing what was going on and doing nothing to stop it and that he was partly responsible for the condition of her daughter because of his inactions. This caused Chief Cramer to sue the newspaper for libel and contemplate having the reporter arrested.

In December 1895, during the trial of the civil suit, Bertha Valentine testified and created a sensation in court, revealing information in regard

Faville building in Dolgeville. *Author's collection.*

to the unsavory mess. She stated that she had improper relations with several young men in the rooms of the dressmaking establishment of Ethel Barger, who induced her to do so. Her testimony included revelations about Chief Cramer trying to persuade her to go with him and his having criminal relations with Nellie Van Ever. Judge McLennan, who, in the middle of the trial, was so angry after learning that Bertha was not even sixteen, summoned the district attorney and had him bring an indictment against Chief Cramer, a man named Frank Johnson and others for rape and against Ethel Barger for abduction for the purpose of prostitution. Numerous other witnesses testified to seeing Chief Cramer with his arm around these young girls walking down Dolge Avenue by the lumber piles. Cramer denied having knowledge that the dressmaking shop was a house of ill repute or that the young girls were prostitutes. The jury in the libel case ruled against Chief Cramer and found a verdict of no cause for action.

Cramer was fired as the chief of police, and a criminal trial for rape proceeded. The girls were subpoenaed to testify by District Attorney Thomas Richardson, assisted by Charles Palmer of Little Falls. While on the stand, Nellie Van Ever dropped a bombshell, stating that on December 23, 1893, Chief Cramer took her to Salisbury. The chief went into the F.C. Ingraham Hotel and brought out some cherry wine to the then-fifteen-year-old child, who drank it. On the way back to Dolgeville, Cramer stopped his cutter, and they got out and had sexual intercourse. Nellie Van Ever further said that Chief Cramer had in the past given her wine at Dolge's Hotel and that she had, on a number of times, sometimes by appointment, "walked the street" with Chief Cramer while he was both on duty and off duty. She also said that he had paid her while she was in the lockup after the trip to Salisbury and received money from other men, but she never received money from the Salisbury trip with Cramer.

Chief Cramer's defense attorneys, A.B. Steele and George Ward, handled the prosecution witnesses roughly. Ward's intention was to show that they were victims and had personal grudges against the defendant. He accused one of them of perjury and intimated that others had bad records. Ward was described as introducing way-back justice court methods into the County Court, and his disregard for the dignity of the court he was in, was unfavorably commented upon.

Elizabeth Cool, the mother of Nellie Van Ever, testified that Nellie's date of birth was June 29, 1878, to confirm that she was only fifteen at the time of the alleged incident with Cramer. She also testified of her history of being married three times, first to Mr. Van Ever; then, about four years prior, to Frank Cool, for seven weeks; and then living with a Mr. Pearl, leaving her daughter behind. When asked by Attorney Steele, "Have you had any more than three husbands?," Mrs. Cool snapped, "No, that's enough, isn't it?" When Steele followed up by asking if she had a divorce from Cool, she laughed and said: "No, I left it with him. When I left him, that was his divorce."

Attorneys Steele and Ward harshly cross-examined witnesses as to the bad reputation of Nellie Van Ever, impeaching their credibility with witnesses of their own and bringing up the arrest of Nellie Van Ever for stealing money from Dr. Clark Getman while employed by him and her improper relations with Fred Lamberson, who was her employer after Dr. Getman. Others, including Martin Gardner and William Helmer, testified as to the bad character of the Van Ever girl.

Chief Cramer, the defendant, testified, and his evidence was substantially the same as in the libel trial. He denied all statements made by Nellie Van Ever as to his alleged relations with her. His wife also took the stand and testified that it was her in the cutter with the wine at the Ingraham Hotel shortly before Christmas two years prior.

Counsel for the people called Bertha Valentine, now using the name Bertha Rose, to the stand, but the court refused to receive the evidence it was intended to present from this witness.

During summation, Attorney Steele asked the jury "to place no dependence in the statements made by the Van Ever girl, who sold herself to men whenever she got the chance." "If such as she is to be believed," he asked, "What may become of mankind? What opportunity is given to drag men down." Counsel reviewed the evidence of Mrs. Cool and said it was no wonder the daughter was so low and depraved. Living in such an atmosphere, she could be nothing but a bad woman.

Charles Palmer summed up that the prosecution had proven beyond a doubt that Nellie Van Ever had gone to Salisbury on December 23, 1893, with James W. Cramer and found it very strange that Van Ever and Mrs. Cramer should tell stories nearly alike about the ride to Salisbury. If it was Mrs. Cramer who was with the defendant, how did Nellie Van Ever know all the details—the time of starting, the drinking of wine at the hotel and the return to Dolgeville? It would appear that the story by Nellie Van Ever was to be most depended on, he said. The defendant, a married man and father of two, could have had only one purpose for taking a little girl, fifteen years old, on that ride and giving her wine. The web that had been woven became untangled.

In the end, Chief Cramer was found not guilty of rape, but the trial left a black mark on the reputations of plenty of prominent young men in Dolgeville who testified in court about the bad character of Nellie Van Ever and exposed the seedier side of a seemingly serene village.

6

THE TROUBLED LIFE
OF ALTON VINCENT

BY JAMES GREINER

Every generation, at any given time, in any community, no matter how big or small, has at least one in their midst. There always seems to be that one person who is either a step ahead of the law or is constantly in and out of jail. In 1900, the city of Little Falls had its fair share of troubled youths, hoodlums and lawbreakers, but one stood out above all others. His name was Alton Vincent.

The 1880 census for Danube summed up the Vincent family in simple terms. John was a farm laborer, while his wife, the former Melinda Fineout, kept house at Fink's Basin. Their first son, Alton, was born on September 22, 1881, and a second son, Edward, was born in 1883.[1]

The quiet farm life the Vincents experienced at Fink's Basin was suddenly shattered in the fall of 1892. Nine-year-old Edward was playing a dangerous game on the railroad tracks with his brother. As a freight train approached, Edward suddenly, at the last minute, darted in front of the engine, only to trip over the second rail. The train lumbered past, crushing both of his legs. Local farmers, hearing the boy scream, carried him home. Doctors were immediately summoned to the Vincent farmhouse, but there was little they could do to save the boy, noting that the severed legs "hung by the skin."[2] The loss of blood, shock to his system and utter exhaustion was more than the small boy could endure. Edward died within hours.

Families deal with the grief of a loved one in different ways. The Vincent family may have tried to erase this awful memory by moving out of Fink's

Basin. In 1893, the family, which included Melinda's ninety-one-year-old mother, Catherine Fineout, traded the rural life of Fink's Basin for the city life of Little Falls. They rented an apartment at 515 Jefferson Street on the south side of the city, across the Mohawk River. Here was the poorest and most congested part of the city. Houses were built so close to one another that it was said if you sneezed in your house, your next-door neighbor said, "God bless you." The move to Little Falls provided more opportunities for the family. John could still find work on the local farms, and Melinda had merely to cross the Mohawk River to find work in one of the many knitting mills. As for twelve-year-old Alton, Little Falls provided opportunities of a different sort.

When Alton lived in Fink's Basin, he probably skipped school on a regular basis and perhaps received a sharp rebuke from his mother and a good spanking from his father. It didn't take Alton all that long to discover that the Little Falls school system was completely different from the one-room schoolhouse he had previously experienced. Throughout the 1894–95 school year, fourteen-year-old Alton Vincent was brought before the city police judge on several occasions, charged with truancy. The stern lecture he received by the police judge had no effect. Alton simply brushed off the affair. Then, with one month remaining in the school year, he was once more before the police judge. Expecting to hear the usual speech, Alton laughed when brought before the judge. After all, what could the judge do? Summer vacation was less than a month away. As it turned out, the judge had the last laugh and sentenced him to reform school—the Rochester Industrial School. Alton was absolutely stunned and broke down in tears. "Vincent's experience," noted the *Little Falls Journal and Courier*, "will serve as a warning to other smart youngsters."[3]

There was no skipping class at the Rochester Industrial School. Alton spent the entire summer there and did not get back home until the first week of September. Standing before the judge with the attorney his mother had hired to secure his release, A.H. Bellinger, Alton assured everyone present that he had learned a valuable lesson. "It's more fun going to school," he assured everyone, than to be locked in at a reform school.[4] The sigh of relief that everyone breathed inside the courtroom turned out to be short-lived, as Alton loved life on the street more than the academic life. Reform school did nothing to reform Alton Vincent. Two months later, in November, Alton, in the company of eleven-year-old Pat Murphy, broke into the livery stable at the Taylor Driving Park a mile west of the city and made off with, according to the press, "everything of value."⁵ After receiving tips from other youngsters in the area, the police brought Alton to the station for questioning. Here, he quickly ratted out Pat Murphy. Holding true to the age-old maxim "There is no honor among thieves," Murphy, when he was questioned, turned on his accomplice. The chief of police determined that both boys were guilty, and the judge agreed. Alton was returned to Rochester Industrial School, and Murphy was sent to St. John's Reformatory in Utica.

By 1900, John and Melinda Vincent had every reason to believe that this last stint in Rochester Industrial School had finally taken effect on their son. Alton was now seventeen years old, had a job at a knitting mill and was taking an interest in his next-door neighbor, Ellen Sweet. However, his mom and dad were mistaken about their errant son. The Jefferson Street gang that Alton was associated with was under constant police surveillance. On several occasions, Alton was brought to the police station, only to be released due to lack of evidence. Few residents of the south side were surprised when petty theft gave way to violent confrontations. In July, the citizens of Little Falls saw a different side of Alton Vincent when Hiram Schuyler swore out a warrant for his arrest. Schuyler claimed that Alton had assaulted his son Raymond. The press no doubt garnered sympathy for Raymond, stating that he was only eight years old while describing Alton Vincent as "a tough youngster who resides on Jefferson Street…an all-around shiftless person and has served a term in the Rochester Industrial School."⁶ What the press failed to mention was that Raymond Schuyler was fourteen years old at the time and apparently no angel. He, too, was an alumnus of the Rochester Industrial School and had an arrest record not quite as long as his assailant. Alton was sentenced to three months in the Albany Penitentiary. After a review of the case, the judge had the sentence suspended.⁷

In April 1901, Alton Vincent was once more in the news and not surprisingly in jail. An angry judge sentenced him to two months in jail for teaching a few local youngsters in Little Falls how to jump trains. It was bad enough that twenty-year-old Vincent had risen to become the premier juvenile delinquent of the city; it was quite another thing to be training the next generation.⁸

Following his release from the county jail, Vincent returned home and, on August 10, married his next-door neighbor, Ellen Sweet. The newlyweds made their new home in what today is 17 Flint Avenue, Little Falls. The responsibility of marriage, the birth of son Edward on November 17, 1901, and his new profession of painting houses may have changed Vincent. Added to this, the family that had seen him through his troubled times was changing. His grandmother Catherine Fineout was living with him, as was his mother, now an "inspector" in one of the knitting mills. Unfortunately, his father was in poor health. He was spending the summer months with the family and the winter months in the soldiers' home in Bath, New York.[9]

In March 1903, William Lassel, a town constable from Indian Castle, arrived at the police station in Little Falls with a warrant for the arrest of Alton Vincent. According to Lassel, Vincent was one of four Little Falls residents wanted for illegal voting in the town of Danube. This was different, thought the Little Falls police, and totally out of character for their favorite felon. Vincent was far more capable of bigger things than this trivial misdemeanor. Not surprisingly, Alton Vincent didn't disappoint anyone.

After searching the side streets of Little Falls, Constable Lassel spotted his quarry on Court Street and immediately placed Alton Vincent under arrest. Alton was cooperative and friendly, and he assured Lassel that he wasn't looking for any trouble. In fact, he asked Lassel if the handcuffs were really necessary. Lassel paused for a brief moment. The charge against Alton carried a fine and not jail time. Feeling confident that Alton was sincere in his promise to behave, Lassel put the handcuffs in his coat pocket. The pair walked several blocks when Alton Vincent saw his chance. He dashed away, and when Lassel drew his revolver and fired two shots in the air, the local press claimed that Alton had "established a new sprinting record."[10]

For several months, Alton Vincent played a game of cat and mouse with the constables of Herkimer and neighboring Otsego County. It seemed that everyone had an "Alton" sighting. On one occasion, Vincent, hiding out in a house owned by Jesse Warren in Richfield Springs, observed two approaching constables. One positioned himself by the front door while the other made his way to the rear of the house. Alton quietly opened a window on the side of the house and, as the press reported, "scampered off over the hills."[11]

Vincent eventually panhandled his way north to Watertown, New York. He was familiar with the area, having worked on the Doner family farm. Enlisting the aid of seventeen-year-old Walter Doner, Alton broke into one barn to steal a horse and another a short distance away to steal a buggy. For almost five months, the two thieves eluded authorities as they crisscrossed northern New York. From Watertown to Gouverneur and back, they robbed local farmers of chickens, oats and vegetables. Their thievery came to an abrupt end when they attempted to steal potatoes. Brandishing firearms during this robbery didn't impress the two field hands, who just happened to be recent Irish immigrants. The Irishmen stood their ground and refused to give up their potatoes. When their border collie lunged at Vincent, the two Irishmen tackled Doner to the ground and beat him senseless. Vincent, "the bigger and more cowardly companion ran away, shooting a shepherd dog that was sent to stop him and grabbed him through the chest. In their flight the two thieves deserted the horse and buggy, which was later recovered by the owners."[12]

Walter Doner was arrested at his mother's home a few days later and sent to the Watertown jail to await trial. Meanwhile, in Little Falls, police had to wait another month to nab their favorite felon. In October 1903, Alton Vincent returned to the wife he hadn't seen or supported in nine months. He was captured while hiding in a kitchen cupboard. One could only hope that his wife received the twenty-five-dollar reward money that was offered for information leading to his arrest.

Found guilty in Herkimer County for illegal voting, Alton Vincent was transferred to Watertown, where he was found guilty of burglary and larceny. Before sentencing him to Elmira Prison, the presiding judge asked him why he did it. Illegal voting wasn't a big issue. Why did you complicate matters by running away and resorting to other crimes? "I don't know," replied Vincent.[13] As usual, he promised to return home a reformed citizen. An editorial in the *Gloversville Daily Leader* wasn't so sure. "Alton Vincent of Little Falls is a young man, but already he has been arrested on the charges of truancy, petit larceny, assault, non-support of his wife, robbery and illegal voting. It must be a great comfort to his [Vincent's] relatives that he has never committed arson."[14] Considering what happened next, his parents probably would have welcomed an arson charge.

After his release from Elmira Prison, Alton Vincent returned to Little Falls and was reunited with his wife and child. To a few neighbors, it did appear as if prison had changed him. Teaming up with one of his hooligan friends from the south side, Alonzo Seeds, Alton returned to the only honest work he knew: painting houses. But, on an all-too-familiar note, he managed to stay out of trouble for only a short while.

In the past, there were probably a few people in Little Falls who delighted in reading of the antics of their resident troublemaker. This came to an abrupt end on one hot summer night in 1908. At about 11:00 p.m. on July 25, the Little Falls police made their way across the bridge that linked the south side to the city. Neither Alton Vincent nor Alonzo Seeds was surprised. The two didn't deny that they had attacked a man on John Street earlier that evening. Alonzo Seeds told the police that they were "two bums from Utica" and that they "had insulted a woman." One of them managed to escape, said Seeds, but the other one got what he deserved. As it turned out, the man they savagely attacked was not from Utica. He was Little Falls native John C. Murphy, fifty-seven. After Seeds and Vincent chased down Murphy, they proceeded to mete out a good beating. This culminated when either Seeds or Vincent took a stone and struck Murphy in the head so hard as to have blood spew from his eye. Horrified neighbors sitting on their porches rushed to the aid of Murphy as Seeds and Vincent fled the scene. Murphy was taken to the hospital, and Vincent and Seeds were taken to the Herkimer County Jail.[15]

On August 5, Sheriff Austin B. Klock had one of those "I have good news and bad news" moments for his latest inmates. The good news, he told Vincent and Seeds, was that the county was dropping the assault charges. The bad news was that they were both being charged with second-degree murder. John C. Murphy, a father of four, had died from complications due to a "fracture of the skull about six inches in length."[16] Witnesses in the jail recalled that Vincent and Seeds "turned pale" when told of Murphy's death.[17]

The prospect of a lengthy prison sentence or the possibility of going to the electric chair weighed heavily on Alton Vincent. When it became known in his circle of cellmates that a hacksaw had been secured, he seized the opportunity to escape. On the night of September 6, 1908, Alton Vincent took part in the largest escape in the history of the Herkimer County Jail. In an incredible breach of security, prisoners that night were not locked in their cells. They had free rein of the enclosed inner cell area. For several days, the prisoners took turns either sawing through the bars or acting as lookouts. That night, snoring prisoners muffled the sound of the last strokes of the hacksaw blade as it cut through the bottom bar to the corridor door. After bending the bar back to secure a ten-to-fifteen-inch opening, six men slithered through the opening and tiptoed down the hall past the other cells. (Cells on the first floor had no access to outside windows.) At the rear of the jail, they performed the same operation. After bending the bar to the side, the six escapees dropped eight feet to the ground below. They were now inside the stockade courtyard in the rear of the jail. There was only one door in the courtyard, and it wasn't locked. It wasn't until 5:00 a.m. that the alarm was sounded.[18]

At first, sheriff's deputies and local police believed that Alton Vincent would be fairly easy to locate. While the Little Falls police questioned his family and searched the south side, other constables were sent to Fink's Basin. Officials in Watertown, who still had his physical description from his

This 1970s overview of the "Historic Four Corners" was taken by Doug Robertson, who was the owner/operator of ROBEL Studios in Herkimer. Note the jail scene. There is the fenced-in yard, which was there when Roxalana Druse was hanged and was still there into the 1970s. The lower window in the back, marked with a drawn square around it, is where the escape took place. The six men lowered themselves to the ground, crept past a sleeping guard and opened the gate, and away they went. *Courtesy of the Village of Herkimer.*

previous arrest, were told to be on the lookout as well. Then, about ten days later, the chief of police received a startling telegram.

> *Chief of Police—I saw Alton Vincent at Groton depot, Massachusetts at 4 o'clock today.*
> *F Champion*[19]

Alton Vincent wore bad luck like a Sunday suit. After successfully eluding the police by traveling in the opposite direction, he was recognized immediately by a boyhood friend as he sat on a railway baggage cart in Groton. He was returned to the Herkimer County Jail and later sentenced to four years and five months at Attica.[20]

While Alton Vincent sat in his jail cell at Attica, his wife, Ellen, took her seat in divorce court. On November 20, 1911, nine days after her divorce was granted, twenty-nine-year-old Ellen Vincent remarried. Her new husband was forty-seven-year-old Joseph Heath. Following a brief honeymoon, the couple, along with Ellen's two children, Edward and George, took up residence on East Jefferson Street in Little Falls.[21]

After his release from Attica (his sentence being extended for a parole violation), Alton Vincent returned to Little Falls with nothing much to show for his life except a long police record and a failed marriage. This last stay in prison mellowed Vincent. The brash young man who flaunted authority was gone. Vincent went back to painting houses; married a widow, Elizabeth Service; reconciled with his two sons; and, for the first time in his life, led a quiet, unassuming life. When he died on May 26, 1962, at the age of eighty-one, few in Little Falls could recall the troubled life of Alton Vincent.[22]

7
THE BACKLASH OF INFIDELITY

BY GREGG LAWRENCE

Sometimes it's not just the economy that makes a business suddenly pull up stakes. Such was the case of the Brambach Piano Factory in Dolgeville. Alois Brambach was one of the most prominent businessmen in town, owner of a successful factory known worldwide at the top of Ransom Street, and he had a beautiful house built (later known as the Menge Complex). But he was married to a woman who was a bit too sociable and enjoyed the limelight as a lavish entertainer.

Elisa Brambach was often seen about town in the company of Dr. William G. Mangold, and the two were a bit more attentive to each other than was becoming. Dr. Mangold also gained entrance to the Brambach residence by making house calls under the guise of the family physician. Seeing Elisa becoming infatuated with him, Mangold encouraged her to break her wedding vows.

The Brambach and Mangold families were at one time on the best of terms, but Alois soon became suspicious of the extra attention between his wife and the doctor, and he threatened Mangold with legal proceedings but was talked out of it by his friends so as to save his wife's reputation. Brambach then confronted Mangold, who acknowledged some fault in the matter and agreed to desist. Alois made arrangements to return Elisa back to her homeland of Germany. In the meantime, unknown to Alois, the affair continued, but it became more discreet. After Elisa returned to Germany, Dr. Mangold continued to correspond with her. Alois came

The Brambach Piano Factory was located on upper Ransom Street, where Gehring Tricot is today. It was in existence from 1892 to 1901. *Editors' collection.*

into possession of one of the letters written by Mangold. The feud reached its boiling point.

On Wednesday, April 17, 1901, Dr. Mangold stepped out of the barbershop next to the post office and was conversing with Attorney J.F. Wilson. Brambach, who had been waiting for his enemy to appear, suddenly pounced on Mangold and brought down on his head with great force the butt end of a whip that he had concealed under his coat. Mangold fell to the sidewalk, and Brambach immediately began applying the lash of the whip on the head of the prostrate man, cutting the doctor with every stroke and drawing blood. The doctor, stunned by the first blow, rapidly recovered and endeavored to offer resistance but was unable to do so to any extent, as his left leg had been injured during the initial encounter. Brambach, however, didn't escape unscathed; while they were struggling, Mangold bit Brambach, badly lacerating his finger and nearly severing it from his hand. The two men, more like wild beasts than human beings, were separated with great difficulty by spectators. It was said that if they had not been separated, they would have killed each other.

Dr. Mangold went to Judge A.L. Leavitt and swore out an arrest warrant on Brambach for second-degree assault. The case was sent to the grand jury. Brambach heard of the proceeding and traveled to Herkimer to meet with the district attorney and surrendered himself, pleaded not guilty and was released on $1,000 bail, his bondsmen being Frank and William Faville.

Back in the village of Dolgeville, Mangold was hanged in effigy with a placard on the figure warning him to leave town. Dr. Mangold was also arrested and out on bail, charged with obtaining money from a widowed woman and keeping it.

The grand jury was convened, and Brambach waited at the Palmer House in Herkimer as the grand jury deliberated. He was then summoned to meet the grand jury, which, in a remarkable scene, not only refused to hand down

WEDNESDAY'S EXCITING ENCOUNTER IN DOLGEVILLE.
ALOIS BRAMBACH AND DR. MANGOLD ENGAGED IN A DESPERATE STRUGGLE

LEADING FIGURES IN THE SENSATIONAL OCCURRENCE OF THE WEEK IN DOLGEVILLE.
MRS. ALOIS BRAMBACH.   DR. MANGOLD   ALOIS BRAMBACH.

Top: *Utica Saturday Globe* (April 20, 1901) depiction of the affray between Brambach and Mangold. *Fultonhistory.com.*

Bottom: Three individuals who became a part of the "wicked" history of Dolgeville. Image from the *Utica Saturday Globe*, April 20, 1901. *Fultonhistory.com.*

an indictment, but also each one of the jury's members shook Brambach's hand, telling him he should have thrashed Dr. Mangold harder.

Although Brambach was vindicated in court, the fact that many in the village, most notably the *Republican* newspaper editor Harry Everest, supported Dr. Mangold, and that many residents felt that his dedication to the welfare of Dolgeville was unappreciated, left a bitter taste in the mouth of Brambach. Within three weeks of the grand jury proceeding, the Brambach factory was empty and the business was relocating to New York City.

A few years later, Dr. Mangold had his own plans to relocate. While he and his wife, Matilda, were in New York City for the holidays, he returned to Dolgeville, leaving her there. Mangold then left a series of letters in their house stating that he was leaving to seek a new home in a strange country and that he had been reckless and that she deserved a better man. He asked for her forgiveness.

After Dr. Mangold was spotted in California by a former Dolgeville resident, Matilda Mangold hired a detective, who traced Dr. Mangold sailing from New York to Panama and then to San Francisco, along with a companion: Elisa Brambach. The eloped couple eventually married, but not for long, as Dr. Mangold died in 1911 at the age of forty-six.

8

THE CHURCH LADY AND THE FOREST RANGER

BY ROBERTA WALSH

In August 1905, Carrie Barnes's name was on every tongue in Fairfield, New York, and not in a good way. When her parents woke up on Saturday, August 5, 1905, they found that Carrie had simply disappeared without a trace. After searching their own house and property, her parents called on the neighbors. None of them had seen Carrie since the day before. But neighbors did report that, at midnight, they had heard a team and rig being driven on the road to Middleville. They noticed it, because that road was rarely traveled between 10:00 p.m. and 4:00 a.m. and the horse was stepping high—stealing the ground right out from under the wheels, as the horsemen used to say.

Carrie would celebrate her twenty-fifth birthday the following month, so she wasn't a child and had every right to go where she pleased. But her parents were worried because of the way that she had disappeared. She had not planned or packed for a trip, and as far as they knew, she carried only some pocket change. But there was no evidence that she had been kidnapped, and nothing was missing from the house or from their property except Carrie herself.

That's when the gossip-festival began.

The day before Carrie disappeared, Charles Klock, the Herkimer County game protector for the State of New York, had boarded the first train to Herkimer. He told his wife that he was going to Albany to consult Chief

Protector Pond on a business matter. When the last train returned on Friday, Klock was not on it.

Charles Klock had worked for the State of New York for some time and was regarded as one of the leading Republicans in Fairfield. He owned a tidy house and had a wife, Emma, and a five-year-old daughter named Beatrice. The only fly in the ointment was that Emma had noticed her husband and Carrie looking at each other in a way that worried her. Emma had actually gone so far as to call on Carrie's mother and suggest that she have a mother-daughter talk about proper deportment between attractive church organists and married men. There is no hard evidence that the supposed infatuation had gone any further than Klock complimenting Carrie's hat or Carrie giving him an extra scoop at the church ice-cream social. But the fact remained that both Charles Klock and Carrie had disappeared within twenty-four hours of each other.

Once the neighbors heard the news, they immediately put two and two together and got five. By Tuesday, August 15, the news had hit the front page of the *Herkimer Citizen* with the headline "Game Protector Klock—Has Skipped the Country with a Young Girl."

Within days, the story had spread from county to county.

Nothing was heard from either Carrie Barnes or Charles Klock until the end of August, when Carrie's parents reported receiving a letter from Parker, South Dakota. Chloe, Carrie's married half-sister, was living in South Dakota with her husband, James Hendrix, and their two children. Chloe reported in her letter that Carrie had just arrived safely in South Dakota after a very enjoyable visit to Chicago.

Two months later, on October 26, Carrie Barnes walked into her parents' house as if she had just stepped out into the yard for a moment to get a breath of fresh air, as if nothing unusual had happened. Carrie had gone to visit Chicago and South Dakota on a whim. That was her story, and she was sticking to it.

Carrie could have gone the rest of her life bearing the brand of a fallen woman. If this had happened in a city, for example Albany or Syracuse, old friends might have stopped speaking to her on the street. But, in Fairfield, the fact that Carrie had apparently gone to Chicago on her own only made her more interesting. Neighbors who had never set foot in the Barnes place now began to drop in to borrow a grindstone or drop off a jar of jam.

But now that Carrie Barnes was home, "safe in the bosom of her family," where in the world was Charles Klock? Certain people were still convinced that Klock and Carrie had run off together, particularly Klock's wife, Emma. But Klock was in trouble with more people than just his wife.

The week before Carrie Barnes turned up back in Fairfield, Harvey Gaylord, the game protector for Lewis County, was arrested on a charge of grand larceny. Although his confession was not made public, newspapers reported that he admitted to Deputy Attorney General Ward that he and Charles Klock had been selling state-owned timber for their own profit.

In New York State at that time, game protectors were responsible for both wildlife and trees. When loggers were allowed to harvest timber on state land, it was up to the game protectors to make sure that they had the proper permits and that they were cutting where allowed.

When three loggers—William Syphert, Albert Harrig and James Gallegher—were caught cutting on state land, they had felled 25,330 trees in the town of Wilmurt (the present-day towns of Ohio and Webb) in Herkimer County. Syphert and Harrig claimed to have paid for a permit and showed the authorities a receipt for $4,000 signed by two game wardens, Gaylord and Klock. Gallegher had a receipt for $3,750. The problem was that these "permits" had never been approved by the proper authorities, and Gaylord and Klock had simply pocketed the money.

New York State Forest, Fish & Game commissioner James S. Whipple is reported to have written a sharp letter to Klock telling him that he had better get this situation straightened out. Klock begged Commissioner Whipple for more time. That was the day, August 5, that Klock had disappeared.

Three months later, on November 4, Charles Klock suddenly reappeared and telegraphed Whipple that he was "ready to face all charges." He said that he had never really been missing at all, that he had suddenly decided to go to Oregon. He wanted to visit the 1905 Lewis and Clark Centennial and American Pacific Exposition and Oriental Fair in Portland, which ran from June 1, 1905, to October 15, 1905. Everyone had heard about the exposition, and 2.5 million people attended. There was even a special forestry exhibit in the world's largest log cabin, where the public witnessed the unveiling of the first sheet of plywood. It was a halfway believable story that was impossible to verify. Klock told the press: "I did not know for weeks after I left Fairfield that charges had been preferred against me. When I did hear of the fact, I began at once to arrange my business to return." He didn't say what kind of business he was arranging or why he left for Oregon without telling anyone where he was going.

Klock's political crony, Sheriff John Richards, posted his bail. Then political shenanigans held up the proceedings for years until a change of leadership in the forestry commission.

In Albany on February 14, 1908, the headline in the *Argus* stated "Game Protector Klock Convicted." Klock was found guilty of grand larceny. Harvey Gaylord had been convicted the week before. Klock served a year in the state prison at Auburn and then went back home to his wife in Fairfield. They may or may not have lived happily ever after. The State of New York never recovered the $7,750.

Carrie Barnes lived in Fairfield for the rest of her life, first with her parents and then with her brother, Clarence. She continued to play the organ for the Fairfield Methodist Church and filled the rest of her time with church activities and good works.

9
FANNY, THE FEMALE FIREBUG

by Roberta Walsh

Fanny had read about criminals in the newspaper. The ones in the newspapers were the ones who had been caught red-handed or who were stupid enough to brag about their crime. Fanny had already figured those two things out. She and Nellie, her partner in crime, had made sure that everything they had stolen was now far away in Pennsylvania, and neither of them had said a word about it to anyone. Even Fanny's husband didn't know the details. But, to make it the perfect crime, the best thing to do would be to make it look like no crime had been committed. Fanny had come up with an idea about how to do that, and Nellie was willing to go along with the scheme.

Fanny Gates came to Herkimer County from Ohio during the summer of 1905. Her husband had gone to Pennsylvania to find a job and to find a house for them to live in. They had rented a nice enough house when they lived in Ohio, but all their furniture had been repossessed because they had never paid for it.

Because Fanny and Nellie were short of money and had no place to live until they moved to Pennsylvania, Lorenzo Kase very generously opened his home to them. Lorenzo was a lumberman, but he did odd jobs in the winter. One of these was caretaker of Alida Burt's home. Alida was a teacher in Champion, New York. Her summer home in Gray was closed up over the winter, so his job was mostly checking for damage from snow and ice.

Fanny and Nellie went to Alida Burt's house for the first time in January. Fanny said later that they had planned to only look in the windows and see how the rooms were furnished. But Fanny saw several things that she would like to have. They climbed in a window and carried out some smaller furniture and a nice carpet that Fanny particularly admired. When Lorenzo Kase wasn't around, they packed the stolen goods in a crate and shipped it to Pitcairn, Pennsylvania. They made two more "shopping trips" to the Burt house and two more shipments to Pennsylvania.

For three weeks, they waited to see if Lorenzo would notice that furniture was missing from the Burt house. Sooner or later he would actually walk around inside the house and would have to notice that something was wrong. Nellie and Fanny grew more worried until Fanny came up with what she thought was an absolutely brilliant plan.

"Why not burn the house down?"

Nellie wasn't sure that burning down the house was such a good idea. She needed some convincing. The ground was covered with snow; how would they hide their tracks? That's when Fanny explained part two of her brilliant plan: They would frame Lorenzo Kase for the arson.

They would walk to the Burt house with Lorenzo Kase's boots tied over their own shoes. The footprints in the snow from Kase's house to the scene of the crime would be Lorenzo's. Fanny planned to start the fire with kindling in one of the bedrooms and have plenty of time to get away. They would go somewhere where they would be seen so they would have an alibi when someone else eventually discovered the fire.

The two women poured some oil on the kindling to help it get started and then touched a match to it. But instead of burning quietly, the kindling burst into flames almost to the ceiling. In a panic, the two women dragged the feather mattress off the bed, hoping that it would smother the fire. But bird feathers are very flammable, and when they're dry, they can burst into flame with just a small spark. Instead of smothering the flames, the feather mattress added fuel to the fire and sent the two women running out of the house. It was February 13, and as Nellie pointed out later, it was not their lucky day.

Within minutes, the women heard the heavy hoofbeats of a team of horses. With no leaves on the trees, a teamster had seen the smoke, had very quickly collected some men and buckets in his wagon and brought them to the fire. The firefighters reported to the district attorney that an accelerant had been used to start the fire, and he called on William Baker of Little Falls to investigate. It was Baker's investigation that led to the arrest of Fanny and

Nellie. They were arraigned before Justice Tompkins, charged with arson in the third degree, burglary in the third degree and grand larceny. When they couldn't post the $1,000 bail set by Tompkins, they went to jail.

Even after they tried to frame him for the arson, Lorenzo Kase didn't believe that Fanny and Nellie were guilty, and he visited them at the jail.

Deputy Sheriff Ingraham, accompanied by Miss Burt, went to Pitcairn, Pennsylvania, looking for the missing furniture. After searching the Gates house, they found nothing and were getting ready to leave when Burt saw a book that she recognized. Inside was the proof they had been looking for: "From Aunt Mary to Alida, Merry Christmas…." They continued searching and found some of Alida's property in a shipping box and two large barrels in a coal shed behind the house.

Fanny Gates and Nellie Perry were arraigned on joint indictments charging arson in the third degree and grand larceny and burglary in the third degree and would be held for trial. Considering all of the evidence against them, they were persuaded that it might be to their advantage to plead guilty and avoid being tried by a jury.

District Attorney Ward accepted their plea of guilty to the indictment of arson, and the two women faced Justice of the Supreme Court William E. Scripture for sentencing. Justice Scripture was sixty-three years old, having come to the court after retiring from his position as postmaster of Rome, New York. Scripture sentenced the women to terms of imprisonment at hard labor in Auburn State Prison for not less than one year nor more than two years and five months.

The next day, Justice Scripture called everyone back into court, saying that he had "reconsidered" the women's sentences. In an unusual move, he reversed his own decision and ordered the original sentencing stricken from the record. Then Scripture re-sentenced Fanny and Nellie to two years each in the state prison at Auburn and one year respectively for each of their crimes. He immediately suspended both their sentences, and the two prisoners simply walked out of the courtroom to freedom.

10

THE HOUDINI OF HORSE THIEVES

by Roberta Walsh

Early Monday morning, April 29, 1908, Justus House, the manager at the Cold Spring Ice Company, discovered a break-in at the Perry Street barn in Little Falls, New York. He reported to police that the company had been relieved of a rig and a team of horses.

Stealing horses was a major crime, so Chief James J. "Dusty" Long, chief of police in Little Falls, telephoned his network of police chiefs with a description of the team and wagon that had been stolen. A tip that came as a result of those phone calls sent Chief Long and Deputy Munsell to Amsterdam, New York, where the horses had been seen in the possession of Mike Brado, also known as "Gypsy Mike." Gypsy is, of course, a derogatory term for the Roma people, who were blamed for stealing horses, much as Italians were blamed for murders and Irish for drunken brawls.

Information gathered in Amsterdam led Long and Munsell to Rotterdam Junction, then to Pattersonville and Schenectady. The tips panned out, and by the first week of May, the horses and rig were on their way back to Little Falls. Gypsy Mike was turned over to Herkimer County sheriff Austin B. Klock. Mike would sit in the Herkimer County Jail with a number of other prisoners for months before he was scheduled to go before the grand jury.

Almost as soon as Gypsy Mike was behind bars, Chief Long and Sheriff Klock started getting calls. A lot of people wanted to get their hands on Gypsy Mike; others wanted to know if any other loot had been recovered.

A pair of sleighs valued at forty dollars had been stolen from James Nichols of Salisbury Center and were found stored in William Thomas's barn, which had been rented by Gypsy Mike.

The horse that Daniel Baynes had left in the drydock barn at Frankfort on November 7 wasn't there when he went back on November 8. Chief Walter I. Bronner of Mohawk thought he saw the same horse ridden through town by Mike Brado, the foreman of a gang of Italians who had been working on the Salisbury railroad. Daniel Baynes was tipped off and headed up the Piseco Road toward Knappville when he spied his horse on a team being driven by Wheeler Knapp. Baynes greeted the horse, the newspapers said, "like an old acquaintance" and reclaimed it. Gypsy Mike had sold the horse to Knapp for $105, which would have been a bargain if he had been able to keep it.

Praime & Bullock complained that Gypsy Mike owed them thirty-eight dollars for feed. Wallace Fish rented out space in his barn for eleven dollars to a stranger who fit the description of Gypsy Mike and who disappeared without paying. George Helterline of Emmonsburg was owed twenty-eight dollars, and Mrs. Liddle in Oppenheim was owed nine dollars.

Reports came in describing harnesses, sleighs, wagons, horses and "diverse other useful and valuable things" that had been swiped by a man named Mike Brado, Napoleon Cote, John Mitchel or Mitchel Jampatsky (all of them fitting Gypsy Mike's description). He seemed to have mowed a swath from Rome to Schenectady before he landed in the hoosegow.

On Sunday, September 6, 1908, Anthony Foster woke up in the Herkimer County Jail. That didn't surprise him, because he'd been arrested for larceny. Bail had been set at $2,500, and he didn't have the money to pay it, obviously, or he wouldn't have been committing larceny in the first place. What did surprise him was that the jail was strangely quiet—and strangely empty.

There were ten cells, five on each side of the corridor. The door to the corridor was locked, but the individual cells were not, allowing the prisoners the use of the corridor. On Saturday, all ten of the cells had been occupied, but this morning, there were prisoners in only four of them. In addition to Foster, the other prisoners still present and accounted for were Edward Murnan, accused of trying to smuggle a hacksaw and map to Canada into the jail for Gypsy Mike; Louis Cavite, charged with burglary; and Alonzo Seeds, who had been implicated in the murder of John Murphy in Little Falls.

A short time later, turnkey (jail guard) Evan Evans was surprised to see prisoner Edward Murnan walking toward him from the street. Murnan had volunteered to crawl out of the opening made by the escaped prisoners and notify someone in authority that the other six prisoners were gone.

Herkimer County sheriff Austin B. Klock sent out descriptions of the prisoners and set rewards of $50 each for either Gypsy Mike or Alton Vincent and $25 for each of the others. These rewards were published in newspapers and amounted to about $1,400 and $700 in today's money, respectively.

> *Michael Brado (Gypsy Mike). Several Other Names—42 years old. Claimed to have been born in Switzerland but is called an Italian. Weight about 165–170 pounds. About 5 feet 4 inches to 5 feet 6. Bald on front part of head. Small turn up nose, light eyes, and wore stubby mustache at time of escape. Talks with a broken accent, and has high pitched voice. Alleged horse thief.*
>
> *Arthur Lighthall (alleged Burglar)—25 years old, weighs about 160 pounds; about five feet seven inches tall; stoop shoulders and has habit of hunching shoulders and blinking eyes when in conversation. Rather heavy head of dark, coarse hair, light eyes, smooth face and has scar under lower jaw (think on right side) caused by an operation. (He was arrested in Utica charged with burglarizing Owen's clothing store.)*
>
> *Alton Vincent (Held on Charge of Manslaughter)—26 years old; weighs 160 to 165 pounds; about six feet tall; rather heavy head of dark hair; dark eyes; small features and smooth face.*
>
> *Elton Praime (Alleged Horse Thief)—32 years old; thick set and weighs about 165 pounds and is about five feet, six inches tall. Not over bright and has rather large, light staring eyes; tousled head of hair and face very much pox-marked.*
>
> *Frank Van Wie (Alleged Burglar)—16 years old; light complexion; medium light hair; blue eyes; smooth face and walks erect.*
>
> *Tony Panza, Italian (Alleged Burglar)—Can give no description of this man other than he is small, wiry built man of 23 years of age and will weigh about 135 pounds. (Arrested & charged with burglarizing the store of Fred J. Tine at Frankfort)*

Arthur Lighthall was picked up by a railroad detective that same afternoon in a boxcar full of tramps in Fonda, New York. One down, five to go. On September 17, Praime and Van Wie were back in jail, caught just outside Little Falls. The next day, Frank Champion was traveling from Herkimer to New Hampshire when he spotted Alton Vincent sitting on a baggage cart in the Groton, Massachusetts station. He had known Vincent since they were boys, so he telegraphed to Little Falls with a positive identification. The constable of Groton, Jerome Chadwick, and the telegraph operator went to the boardinghouse where Vincent was staying and put him under arrest. The judge split the reward three ways. Constable Chadwick should have fifteen dollars, the telegraph operator fifteen dollars and Champion twenty dollars.

With Vincent back behind bars, two prisoners were still on the run: Tony Panza and Gypsy Mike. When he was questioned, Vincent told Sheriff Klock that he had last seen Gypsy Mike in Mechanicsville, about eighty miles east of the jail. Gypsy Mike's case came before the grand jury on December 8, and Deputy Sheriff Munsell went to Herkimer, just in case. But, of course, Mike didn't show up.

Gypsy Mike was the burr under Sheriff Klock's saddle. The sheriff never quite gave up hope that Mike would be caught. People still hoped to claim the reward, and reports that Gypsy Mike had been spotted came in from time to time, but none ever panned out.

POSTSCRIPT: IN JANUARY 1909, Sheriff Klock got a tip from someone who claimed that Gypsy Mike was at a lumber camp in Canada and that he could lead Klock right to it. The sheriff did not waste a single minute packing a bag and buying a train ticket, so eager was he to put Gypsy Mike before the grand jury. An hour later, the sheriff got a phone call from the tipster telling him that it was all a big joke. An hour or so after that, the Reverend Ure Mitchell was on his way to the home of a local clergyman to make arrangements to deliver a talk at his church. Mitchell was a stranger in Herkimer, a former Congregational minister who was in charge of excursion trains from Montreal to the shrine of Sainte-Anne-de-Beaupré. As a tour guide and public speaker, he was often asked to talk at various churches and at meetings of clubs and ladies' groups. This unfamiliar face was spotted by a deputy, who mistook him for the practical joker and decided to arrest him on suspicion. Reverend Mitchell told the deputy that if he did not have a warrant for his arrest, he had better let him go. Mitchell was allowed to go on his way. Five minutes later, he met up with Sheriff Klock, who also tried to arrest him! Their raised voices attracted a crowd. Mitchell appealed to his audience; eventually, the sheriff was persuaded to go to the house of the clergyman, with the crowd tagging along, where Reverend Mitchell was able to prove that he was who he claimed to be.

11

WHEN YEGGS HIT HERKIMER COUNTY

by David Waite

While not a banner headline, being on the front page of the *Ithaca Daily Journal* was more than enough for this bold caption to catch the attention of even the most casual reader:

YEGGMEN DISPLAY COLOSSAL NERVE
Kidnap Mohawk Policeman and Coolly Loot Post Office

It was late on Wednesday, January 19, 1910, and Police Chief Walter I. Bronner was making his evening rounds through the quiet village of Mohawk, making sure all was safe for both business and residents. Someplace near the intersection of Main and Washington Streets, he encountered four men, who engaged him in conversation as they all walked along. Before he could resist, Bronner was relieved of his pistol, gagged and brought into the Masonic Hall billiards room that the Yeggs had broken into earlier in the evening. Once inside, Bronner was bound with wire taken from pictures on the wall.

The Masonic Hall shared a building with the village post office, so it was a simple matter for the Yeggmen to gain access to that office's safe. Still bound and gagged, Officer Bronner was given a front-row seat as the burglars placed explosives and blew open the safe. Surprisingly, no one took notice of the blast, and the Yeggs quickly disappeared with about

A photo of Chief Walter Bronner (1862–1944) in his later years standing in front of the Columbia Street School. (This site now is Mohawk's municipal building.) He was Mohawk's police chief for thirty-five years (1902–37). *Courtesy of Herkimer County Historical Society.*

$200 in stamps and cash. An hour after they had made their escape, Bonner was able to get free and sound the alarm. Though a posse was quickly formed, no clues were found to indicate what direction the men might have headed.

The Story of John Yegg

While some experts in the language of criminal behavior have attempted to tie the name *Yegg* to vague references to tramps from the past, the most reasonable origin is revealed in a story of the life of one John Yegg, though even that leans more toward urban legend than historical accuracy.

With the colorful title "Swedish Desperado," John Yegg first surfaced somewhere in the Pacific Coast states in the late 1870s. Yet the story truly begins thousands of miles away and some twenty years before, at the laboratory of a world-renowned scientist. In 1847, the Italian chemist Ascanio Sobrero synthesized the powerful chemical nitroglycerin. Due to its unstable elements, he strongly urged against its use as an explosive. Soon, the scientist Alfred Nobel began developing the substance as a commercial explosive. After his brother Emil and several others were killed while manufacturing this highly unstable chemical in 1864, Nobel moved the operation to an isolated factory near Hamburg, Germany. It took another three years and several deadlier accidents before a more stable form of this explosive, dynamite, was developed by mixing nitroglycerin with diatomaceous earth.

Soon after the Civil War, the U.S. government began investigating nitroglycerin for both commercial and military use. Unfortunately, the results of these experiments, published and widely distributed, included successful tests on burglar-proof safes. It is here that the urban legend of John Yegg and the history of those named for him begins.

John Yegg came from one of the western states and was said in his time to have been one of the most experienced and expert electrical mechanics in that part of the country. The story goes that due to excessive drink, he fell into a life of crime that led from simple robbery to blowing open safes using the slow and tedious process of drilling and dynamite. Learning of nitroglycerine's power, and with rough instruction provided by the government, he soon perfected both the method of extracting nitroglycerine from dynamite and an effective procedure for breaking open a safe. Of course, he was more than willing to share his secrets—so much so that, soon, safecrackers across the country were finding a new level of success in their illegal endeavors.

Before I get into the secrets that John Yegg is said to have so freely passed along, there is an equally important factor that greatly contributed to a Yegg's success. He lived a life in many ways similar to a freight-train-hopping tramp. By using the railroad for transportation, these bandits could travel unseen into nearly every area of the state and then quickly leave again, heading wherever a passing freight car would carry them. Unlike the worn clothing of an average hobo, a Yegg often wore clothes similar to that of an average mechanic or day laborer of the time.

To successfully pull off their robberies, the Yeggs would form gangs, sometimes coming together only for a specific job, or more often as groups that gathered around a known and successful mastermind. A gang usually consisted of two "inside men," who broke into the post office or other business that was being robbed, and one or more "outside men," who watched out for police or village watchmen. Additionally, the gang often had someone whose job it was to obtain details of the place they were planning on hitting. This was either a child, called by the Yeggs a "kitten," or an adult member of the gang, a "gay cat." They were sometimes disguised as an invalid selling pencils or other small items door to door. They then tried to gain unnoticed access to the inside of the building to be robbed.

As nitroglycerine was rarely available in a quantity that a Yegg needed to open a safe, the most skilled operator in a gang would extract the nitroglycerine from the inert material in dynamite, which made the explosive relatively safe and stable. At a hobo camp along a railroad, a fire was built, and dynamite stolen from a construction project was heated in a can of hot water until the nitroglycerine rose to the top. Given the name *soup* by the Yeggs, it was normally put into a pint- or smaller-sized rubber container; when nothing else was available, a household quart jar was used. In glass, the extremely unstable nitroglycerine was prone to explode if shaken or jarred, and the death of one or more gang members from an unexpected explosion was not uncommon. The chemical nitroglycerine had another property that added to its danger: its freezing point was around fifty-five degrees, requiring it to be kept close to the body in cool weather.

Once the inside men broke into a business—commonly a village post office not far from the railroad—the work of preparing the safe commenced. A bar of soap was softened and spread around the edge of the door of the safe, making a channel for the nitroglycerine. At the top, a cup was formed, and the explosive was slowly poured in. When the channel was full, a fuse was attached. Sometimes, rugs or heavy blankets were spread across the safe to muffle the sound. Then the fuse was lit. If all went well, the blast opened the safe, and any money, stamps or change was removed. Safe manufacturers responded to these attacks, and new safes were built that sometimes required two or three explosions to open. There was also the chance that too much nitroglycerine was used, and the safe, its contents and the building itself were destroyed.

With the safe opened and emptied, the gang would beat a very hasty retreat, often in a stolen wagon or automobile, to the closest passing freight train. If during their flight from the scene of the crime any citizen or police intervened, the gang would not hesitate to shoot their way to freedom.

One important part of the Yeggs' lifestyle was their disinterest in accumulating wealth and living "high on the hog" from the proceeds of their burglaries. After a successful robbery, it was not abnormal for a gang to head to a tavern miles from the scene of the crime and spend all their loot getting

Stevensville Montana Western News, September 26, 1900. Yeggman illustration 2.

"YEGGMAN" PLIES HIS VOCATION.

drunk. When a gang had been exceptionally successful, they were known to simply throw all their money on the bar and invite anyone present to help drink up the proceeds.

Even when following the established methods of burglary and blowing safes, there was no guarantee of success. In the autumn of 1895, a group of Yeggs broke into the post office in the Herkimer County village of West Winfield. After blowing the safe, the thieves got away with only ten dollars in cash. After the break-in, the postmaster was relieved to find that the unlocked money drawer filled with cash and stamps had not been disturbed. The Yeggmen had stolen a horse and carriage for their escape, fled to Ilion and there boarded a freight train leaving the area.

As federal detectives became better equipped to pursue and capture these criminals, and as safe manufacturers improved their products to thwart their schemes, the attacks on post offices in rural communities greatly diminished. By the 1920s, it was rare when the local paper reported news of a band of these bandits bringing their acts of mayhem to a local community, and the term *Yegg* quickly fell out of use.

12

THE TEXTILE STRIKE RIOT

BY ANGELA HARRIS

> *On October 9, 1912, out of 1,100 textile workers employed by the Phoenix Knitting Company at Little Falls, 80 went on strike against a reduction in wages caused by the operation of the fifty-four-hour law. The operation of this law, in effect on October 1, prohibited the employment of women or minors for more than 54 hours in any one week. On October 18, 76 out of 495 employed by the Gilbert Knitting Company joined in the strike.*

The dry opening paragraph of the Report from the New York State Department of Labor on the Little Falls Textile Strike of 1912 barely suggests the complex threads in the U.S. economic and social evolution that, woven together, produced a three-month event affecting the whole city of Little Falls.

The city experienced major economic growth between 1895 and 1910, with circular knitting a major industry. With this came the demand for workers. Historically, the population of Little Falls had been of English, Irish and German ancestry. But as the total population in the city increased from 9,897 in 1895 to 12,273 in 1910, the immigrant population grew commensurately. The new residents came primarily from Italy, Poland, Slovakia and Slovenia. These immigrants lived in crowded quarters on the south side of the Mohawk River and Canal, separated from the established citizens by language and ethnic background as well as geography.

In the first week of October, working hours for women were reduced from sixty a week to fifty-four a week in the State of New York. The operative legislation resulted directly from the Second Report of the Factory Investigating Commission, which had been created in response to the Triangle Shirtwaist Fire in New York City on March 25, 1911. This tragedy resulted in 146 deaths and 78 injuries, mostly young women and mostly immigrants between the ages of fourteen and twenty-three. Many jumped to their deaths; others succumbed to smoke or flames. But the tragedy inspired lawmakers to address the implications of industrialization. The first concrete result was the fifty-four-hour workweek for women, which went into effect on October 1.

The first major ripple from the reduction in hours was the corresponding reduction in pay. At the Phoenix Mill, eighty women walked out over the pay loss. They were soon joined by fifty-six from the Gilbert Mills. By the end of the month, between two hundred and three hundred marchers joined the picketing every day. Some were strikers, and some were sympathetic workers displaced by understaffing and subsequent work reduction.

Within days of the walkout, the strikers were joined by sympathetic socialists from Schenectady led by Mayor George Lunn. The socialists held rallies at Clifton Park, across the street from the train station, and rapidly their concerns moved to a defense of free speech after several were arrested for assembling in a public space without the appropriate permits. Police Chief James "Dusty" Long had wasted no time and arrested Lunn and the other Schenectady representatives on October 13 and held them for questioning overnight.

On the same day, newspapers throughout the state headlined the level of threat to the city and strikers alike. The *New York Herald* headed a report with this caption: "Strike of 30,000 Mill Workers Is Threatened at Little Falls." The number suggested was overblown and inflammatory and clearly had not been provided by local observers, who had a better grasp of what was happening.

The city fathers were, of course, predisposed to object to the strikers. Any limit or shutdown of production in the mills that made Little Falls an industry center in the state of New York hurt the economy. And from the beginning of the labor action, the distrust of the "foreigners" by the longtime residents of the city was evident. Long revealed the kind of society the city fathers had fostered and were interested in controlling.

In a statement issued on October 18, Chief Long encapsulated the position taken by the city "leaders." "We have a strike on our hands and a foreign element to deal with. We have in the past kept them in subjugation and we mean to continue to hold them where they belong. We will not allow anyone to attempt publicly to stir up a feeling which might cause serious trouble to this city, county, and state....The city may have these local quarrels, but I will at all times object to butters-in" (*Amsterdam Evening Recorder*, October 18, 1912).

The strikers appealed to the International Workers of the World, also known as the IWW or the "Wobblies." The IWW sent Benjamin Legere, a spokesman and organizer, to Little Falls. Legere helped the strikers set up a committee of twenty-four persons to coordinate activities.

With each passing day, the strikers became more organized, and as support increased from the IWW and socialists from Schenectady, the lines were drawn in the city.

Chief James "Dusty" Long (1864–1944) served with the Little Falls Police Department as its chief for thirty-five years (1905–40). *Courtesy of Little Falls Historical Society.*

The days had developed a pattern. The strikers assembled at the strike headquarters in rented space at the Slovak Hall on German Street. The building was the home of the Slovak social clubs. Every morning, the strikers met at 6:00 a.m. to march across the nearby Bellinger Street Bridge (no longer standing) to the strike site on South Ann Street. The morning march was usually an upbeat affair. The strikers hired the Slovak Band to lead the march. As it played, the strikers sang, sometimes in their native languages and sometimes in rousing versions of the "La Marseillaise," which had become the international workers' hymn. Often, the day's march leaders carried a red flag. At lunch, the picketers returned to the Slovak Hall, where the strike committee had set up a soup kitchen.

Typically, the marchers would picket, walking in a large circle in front of the mills on Ann Street and Mill Street. They continued as the nonstriking workers arrived for work. The strikers would also assemble in Clifton Park, especially at lunchtime, when speakers such as Mayor Lunn would fire up the strikers, talking about workers' rights, free speech and the socialist vision for citizens in a socialist world.

By October 16, the strike had spread to include the Gilbert Mill on Mill Street, down the block from the Phoenix Mill. That mill was reported dark

Slovak Hall on German Street (now Flint Avenue), where the strikers had their headquarters. *Courtesy of Little Falls Historical Society.*

on that night. Mayor Lunn and his compatriots from Schenectady continued to argue their right to speak in the public park with a larger audience.

The strikers made a formal request to the management of the mills, asking for a restoration of the weekly wages from the time of the sixty-hour week. Simply, they wanted to earn the same weekly total they had before the state imposition of a shorter workweek. The demands were expanded to include changes in the parameters and pay of night-shift workers. There were arrests and hearings but, to that point, no sign of violence. Antagonism grew between the sides, but it was distressing rather than dangerous.

On October 17, Helen Schloss, the local contagion nurse, resigned her position in the city and joined the strikers. She had been hired by the Fortnightly Club, a women's club whose members were primarily of the owner and management class. Schloss had come to Little Falls to work on the tuberculosis problem. She had arrived at the beginning of the summer, and her work took her into the mills and the tenements. Her commitment to the work and her history of socialist involvement led her to leave the employ of the sponsoring club and work directly with the strikers.

In the early days of the walkout, the strikers were joined by workers who had been idled by the strike, along with usually 200 to 300 marchers every day. Over the duration of the labor action, as many as 800 were on strike and as many as 1,500 mill employees were out of work. Tensions between strikers and the rest of the city increased with each day.

Over time, the police under the direction of Chief Long stood by for the morning marches and midday rallies. The issue of freedom of speech was resolved so that the socialists could continue to speak at rallies. By the end of October, rumors of potential violence, coupled by longtime distrust, led Long to call in Sheriff James W. Moon from Herkimer and, subsequently, a private police force from Albany. Law enforcement was ready for trouble.

Then came October 30. It's not clear whether that day's riot resulted from a plan, a rash action or a mistake.

On the morning of the thirtieth, the march started as usual, with a meeting of the strikers in Slovak Hall. There are no reports of the morning meetings, but there is nothing to indicate that the pot was being stirred and that trouble was inevitable. Certainly, tension was evident in the relationship between the strikers and the police. And even before the riot, Mayor Lunn had been charged with "inciting to riot" and jailed awaiting trial. Everyone recognized the volatility of the strike situation, but the strikers were not deterred.

There was nothing particularly ominous about that morning: Leaving the Slovak Hall singing and marching, several hundred mill workers crossed the Bellinger Avenue Bridge led by the Slovak Band on their way to picket in front of the Phoenix and Gilbert Mills on South Ann and Mill Streets. As usual, strikers sang as they marched. They reached the picketing site by 6:30 a.m., but not long after the marchers reached South Ann Street, there was trouble.

As had been their practice, the strikers marched in a large circle that was reported to have blocked access to the Phoenix Mill for those still working. At that point, it seems that everything went to hell. Reports are, of course, confusing. No cell-phone cameras existed to record what happened. There are a few photos, but mostly there are the conflicting reports. And, not surprisingly, the reports were slanted by the reporters, be they traditional city and police loyalists or strikers and their union and socialist supporters.

As for what ignited the confrontation, some say the strikers made a circle in front of the mill access so that workers had to walk through the strikers' line twice. Other reports say that the strikers lined both sides of the sidewalk. At this point, reports become even more muddled and contradictory, especially regarding who started it. Chief Long was at the site at 6:30 a.m. when the strikers arrived. Prepared for trouble, he was accompanied by members of the Little Falls Police Department and hired private police from the Humphry Agency in Albany. He may have entered the strikers' circle in an attempt to move or disband it. He pushed a striker, or a striker pushed him, and the melee erupted. Some subsequent reports declare that the strikers threw stones at the police and that when they were arrested they all had pockets full of stones.

Several details were consistent throughout the reporting. Long was hit in the head by a rock. A special policeman from Albany was slashed around the neck and head by a knife-wielding striker, reported by some to have been a woman. About two dozen officers waded into the crowd of strikers with their clubs, some picketers being knocked unconscious. A shot was fired—with a local police officer shot in the leg. As many as twenty strikers were beaten by the police with their clubs. Both of the injured officers were taken to the local hospital and recovered completely, but there were no reports on the injured strikers. Long called for support from Sheriff Moon in Herkimer.

The strikers dispersed, and many ran back across the river to their homes and to Slovak Hall. Long and his officers set out to identify and arrest the strike leaders with the intent of blaming the skirmish on them. In the first few hours after the confrontation, over thirty people were arrested, including strikers and union organizers. Helen Schloss was arrested, even though she wasn't at the picketing that morning. She still lived on the north side of the river, up the hill from the mills, and spent her days at the strike headquarters. She was intercepted by one of the strikers before she made her way to the site and was informed of what was happening. She turned, instead, to the post office, which had a public phone. Captain Long arrested her on the building steps before she was able to contact anyone.

The police chief and his force, supported by the private force from Albany, were joined by the sheriff and his officers. Some of the Little Falls police pursued the strikers to the headquarters. What followed is reported differently by the two sides. According to the police and

Helen Schloss. *Courtesy of Little Falls Historical Society.*

city fathers, the police, in pursuit of miscreants and weapons, pushed people from the steps of the hall and broke the doors to enter. They searched the facility and found evidence of the strikers' state of mind, according to the mayor.

According to the *New York Call* (a socialist publication): "Squads of special thugs who were brought into this city from Albany were sworn in today by Sheriff Moon of Herkimer County as special deputies and were supplied with guns and clubs. They are in possession of the city and refuse to permit the strikers near the mills."

The *Utica Herald-Dispatch* of October 31, 1912, reported:

> Search of Slovak Hall this morning discovered, besides a musket and a sword already mentioned, 32 beer cases, 9 empty and 23 filled. Besides those there was an empty beer barrel. There was also 9 cases of empty soft drinks and 5 empty whiskey bottles in addition to 2 partly filled whiskey bottles.
>
> The authorities believe that the discovery explains to a great extent this morning's trouble. The police have seized all of this property and are holding it at headquarters.

On the other hand, the paper continued, "A committee…representing the Gymnastic Slovak Union School," sent a statement to the local newspapers.

> We feel hurt that the officers of the law entered and so ruthlessly desecrated our club rooms which we had been able to build and furnish by dint of many personal sacrifices, in order that we might have a place to gather in social intercourse evenings and enjoy ourselves as we did in our native country.…We sublet our gymnasium to the strike committee, the same as they might have rented any other public hall. The beer taken from the hall was club property and we had a club license, which was also taken away in the raid. The reason for such a quantity was that we purchased by wholesale.…The empty whiskey bottles, over which they made so much fuss, the old bayonets, the sword and guns all were used in our gymnasium as property for our amateur performances.

By the end of the day, all twenty-four members of the strike committee, along with several of the Schenectady socialists and known strike supporters, were arrested, but Ben Legere was not yet found. The Little Falls Jail was inadequate for the numbers arrested and lacked accommodations for women to be held separately from men. All in all, thirty-one strikers were arrested and taken to the jail in Herkimer. Ben Legere and several other leaders were not immediately found, but local leaders, including Helen Schloss, and the Schenectady supporters were among those sent to Herkimer. Legere was arrested on November 1 and charged with assault for an attack on a police officer during the riot.

For several weeks, the police and judges sorted out the charges and bail for the strikers and socialists. But local leaders were fed up with the interruption in their lives and business. More than two hundred merchants in the city called for a general meeting of the community to address the problems facing the city. Religious and community leaders spoke at the general meeting held at the Hippodrome on November 6. Most of the speakers abhorred the violence of the riot and the disruption of the economy in the city. Since from the very beginning of the action strike support had come to Little Falls from around the state and county, it was easy for the city fathers to blame much of the trouble on "outside influences."

The strikers received little support from the "American" workers. Some of the immigrants had been brought to the city to break a strike that these same strikers had initiated several years before. The strike was not a two-sided disagreement but rather a multifaceted mess. The city fathers, mill owners and religious leaders were committed to a form of status quo. The "American" mill workers, immigrant mill workers, socialists, the IWW and the AFL (American Federation of Labor) were fighting to represent the workers.

On November 9, Schloss was released on bond after being examined by a committee of three doctors whose task it was to determine her sanity. Strike leaders and participants were still being arraigned, but the threat of violence seems to have abated. At about that time, Mathilda Rabinowitz, an IWW organizer from Connecticut, arrived in Little Falls and took over the work of the departed or jailed leaders. She rented a room on Jefferson Street not far from the strike headquarters and went to work.

Big Bill Haywood also arrived in Little Falls to work with the strikers. But primarily he traveled around the state giving speeches to make money to support the workers. The strike continued, but with all twenty-four of the elected strike committee members and several of the professional union workers in jail, things began to change.

The state labor board became involved, and immediately the mill owners refused to negotiate as long as the IWW was involved. The mill owners, with the support of the police, hired nonstrikers and refused to hire back strikers. Miscommunication of malicious intent or misunderstanding marred attempts at resolution, and it became a fight between unions to represent all the workers in the Phoenix and Gilbert Mills.

On December 24, State Labor Commissioner Williams directed the Board of Mediation and Arbitration to conduct a public inquiry at Little Falls. The hearings and findings were reported in the Little Falls Textile Workers' Dispute statement.

The riot did not bring an end to the strike or to the commitment of the strikers to a restoration of their pre-fifty-four-hour-week pay. But it was the involvement of the State Board of Mediation that finally resolved the labor action. On December 27, 28 and 30, 1912, at the Common Council Chamber, Little Falls, testimony showed that the main cause of the strike was the pay reduction after the implementation of the fifty-four-hour week. The final agreement (1) restored the previous salaries, (2) guaranteed freedom from recriminations by management, (3) reinstated former employees, (4) adjusted the piecework rate and (5) made some technical stipulations related to "winding schedules" of yarn.

The workers met on January 2 and voted to accept the resolution and return to work on January 6, 1913.

The strike was over. The riot was a sour memory, the true details of which never became really clear.

13

THE CASE OF THE RAT-FINK ROOMMATE

by Roberta Walsh

Almon Cole had a job at the TNC Garage in Watertown, New York. It was not a bad job at all, but money was a little tight. To make ends meet, he took an apartment with a roommate. Splitting the rent seemed like a good idea at the time. The roommate was George Wallace. He was twenty-eight years old and working in Michael Farone's barbershop. Cole was happy to find that he could also convince Wallace to loan him a little money.

Sharing an apartment with Wallace went OK for a while, but then, one night in April 1921, Almon Cole, for reasons of his own, decided to share his dirty little secret: "I've killed a man." Wallace just sat there, probably stunned, but still listening, so Cole told him that he had been driving from Ilion to Frankfort some time earlier when he was distracted by a low-flying airplane near the Union Fork and Hoe factory. Watching the plane instead of the road, he hit a man. He drove away, leaving the man lying by the railroad tracks. Wallace asked, "How do you know he was dead?" Cole told him, "It was in the papers the next day."

If you want to lead a life of crime, you need to know the people in whom it is safe to confide. George Wallace was not one of those people. He didn't remember the details, but a couple of years prior, there had been a hit-and-run accident in Frankfort, and the family of the dead man offered a $1,000 reward for information leading to the arrest of the driver. (That's over $14,000 in today's money.) Wallace would be a rich man, and the apartment would be all his!

The details of that hit-and-run actually added up to a very annoying cold case for the Frankfort police. In November 1919, a body had been found near the railroad tracks in Frankfort. The coroner, Ralph Huyck, had ruled the death accidental. The well-dressed young man had gotten his head bashed in, he decided, while trying to "hop a freight" for a free ride. The body was tentatively identified as that of traveling salesman Clarence Kelly, and his family in Rochester was notified. Clarence's brother George was sent to identify the body. George was angry and confused when he was told that Clarence had died while trying to "hop a freight." George knew his brother better than anyone and thought this explanation was totally insane. Clarence always wore a suit and tie and had never been the least bit athletic. He would never have been running to jump on a train like a hobo. And where were his suitcases? Clarence never traveled with fewer than two. Clearly, the coroner had either made an honest mistake or, as George suspected, had decided not to waste anyone's time solving the murder of someone from out of town. George finally managed to convince the police that his brother's death might not have been an accident. He brought in his own investigator, Detective Doyle, from Rochester and offered a $1,000 reward for information leading to the arrest of his brother's killer.

Wallace went to the Watertown police station and told Chief of Police Edward J. Singleton what he knew: that his roommate, Almon Cole, had confessed to hitting a man with his car near Frankfort and leaving the body near the railroad tracks. The chief immediately connected it with Clarence Kelly's death and notified Detective Doyle at Rochester to come to Herkimer County. In the meantime, Chief Singleton had Cole brought in and started questioning him. Cole admitted that he had told Wallace a story about killing a man but insisted none of it was true.

Cole was put under arrest and taken to Herkimer, where he was questioned for some time. He eventually admitted that some of what he had told Wallace might be true. Over and over again, they asked him, "Did you, Almon Cole, run down a man with your car near the railroad tracks near Frankfort in November 1919?" Detective Doyle admitted that he didn't know what to make of Cole and that he was losing hope of ever making sense of his conflicting stories. But finally, Cole's answers started making sense. Yes, he had run down a man with his car, and yes, it was near the railroad tracks; but no, it was not in November 1919. It was the night of August 31, 1918.

Almon Cole's confession left the police scratching their heads. Now they had a killer for a crime that hadn't been committed. There was no record of a hit-and-run accident on August 31, 1918, but a body had been reported. Coroner Dr. Edward B. Manion investigated the death of George Martin Curry, an employee of Remington Arms in Ilion, and recalled that the man had been struck by the trolley that ran between Frankfort and Herkimer. Although it wasn't entirely clear how it had happened, the death had been declared accidental.

Almon Cole was charged under Section 290 of the Highway Law for leaving the scene of an accident, narrowly escaping the possible charge of manslaughter. Detective Doyle went back to Rochester, haunted by the Clarence Kelly murder for the rest of his life. The reward offered by the Kelly family went unclaimed, and the murder was never solved. And, finally, a sadder and wiser George Wallace went back to his apartment without the $1,000 reward and without a roommate to split the rent.

14

ORGANIZED CRIME IN HERKIMER COUNTY

By Patrick J. Luppino

Prior to the unification of Italy, the island of Sicily often existed under the oppression of other countries and rulers. Over time, the population of Sicily started to form groups to help fight off other countries. These groups quickly started to use their power with negative methods and formed their own style of practices. Sicily became an increasingly violent island, and small, military-style factions started to exploit this. These groups, known as "Mafie," or what we know today as the Mafia, used their power to oppress the people of Sicily. The influence of the Mafia quickly began to rise across the country, and organized crime became a major part of Italy's history.

Since the United States continued to be viewed as a land of opportunity, many Italians with influence in the Mafia started to settle in major cities. The 1920s was a perfect time to immigrate to the United States. The Italian fascist dictator Benito Mussolini attempted to dissolve the Mafia, which he viewed as a threat to his plan to rise to power in Italy. Along with this, the Eighteenth Amendment was ratified, prohibiting the manufacture, transportation and sale, but not the consumption, of alcohol in the United States. This period, known as Prohibition, gave the Mafia a suitable product to profit from. Many groups and families started smuggling alcohol into the United States from Canada and manufacturing homemade alcohol in hidden distilleries. Prime locations for such activity were the major cities close to the Canadian border, including Chicago and New York City. These cities also participated in the luxurious and partying lifestyles of the Roaring Twenties. Alcohol in these cities was a necessity for clubs to keep up with the lifestyle. Along with the smuggling of alcohol, illegal gambling, extortion, racketeering, as well as murder, cover-ups and power grabs in communities continued, mostly in Italian-populated areas.

While the Mafia existed in many parts of Upstate New York, in the cities of Buffalo, Syracuse, Utica and Albany, the crime was the worst. A small group of wrongdoers worked in and around the town of Herkimer. The earliest recorded activities took place in the late 1910s by a group calling itself the "Herkimer Black Hand Gang." The gang used the Black Hand symbol of extortion to terrorize the people of Herkimer's and Frankfort's Italian communities. The records of these men give little detail about their lives outside of being arrested.

Beginning in the middle of 1906 and ending in early 1907, Joseph Crubi, the alleged leader of the gang, and his followers would attempt to extort money from Italian Americans. There is little information about Joseph Crubi prior to his arrest, but he was around twenty-three years old at the time. The year of his immigration and any other information pertaining to his life was never recorded or is unknown. The same is true of a few of his followers who were also arrested.

These men would leave letters marked with the Black Hand symbol and worded with fancy or Old English–styled sentences. They would also knock on the doors of residents of the Italian communities, like William Street in Herkimer. Joseph Crubi and his followers used to threaten these residents with violence against themselves, their families or their possessions. Eventually, in early 1907, Crubi and a few of his followers were arrested. Crubi was sentenced to sixteen years in Auburn State Prison, but it is unknown if he served the full term, and it is not known what happened to him after his time in jail. A few of his followers avoided jail time by promising to leave Herkimer County. Again, nothing is known about them afterward.

Years after Joseph Crubi's Black Hand Gang, more organized crime moved into the area. Located just outside of Utica—nicknamed "Sin City" or "The City that God Forgot" because of the amount of organized crime in these periods—Frankfort and Herkimer continued to serve as hotspots for organized crime and smuggling. The two towns are found along one of the smuggling routes from Canada, contributing to their own histories and to the history of their roles in Prohibition. The area was never as wild as Utica, but proximity to the city allowed the gangs in these cities to use the area well into the late twentieth century.

Along with smuggling, many murders related to organized crime took place in this area. One story tells about a non-Italian man in Herkimer's Italian community using a racial slur against a group of kids playing around with his truck. In the following days, he ended up gunned down in his own truck in the same area for "an unknown reason." Due to privacy concerns, the names and the source of the story donated to the Herkimer County Historical Society will remain undisclosed.

The *Ilion Citizen* of December 12, 1907, recounts the murder on Main Street in Frankfort of Guiseppi Skran, who was shot three times by Joseph Dove after Skran and others had issued threats demanding money of Dove a week before. Skran implored that he did not have the money, but the gang members pressed home their threats with a "wicked looking knife" and said they would "cut off Mr. Dove's head and his wife's head and would blow up his house." These threats were followed up with several letters. Dove sent word to the local police chief, J.S. Getman, telling him to prepare to defend himself. On Saturday, December 7, Dove ran into Skran at Joseph Lombardo's saloon and followed him outside, demanding the money. Dove opened his pocketbook, showing that it was empty, but declared to Skran that he had something else, pulling out a revolver and shooting three times. One bullet passed through Skran's lungs. Skran ran back into the saloon, where he fell. Chief Getman was nearby and ran to the scene. Dove recounted what had happened and gave the names of other Italians associated with Skran. One of them was arrested and taken to the Herkimer jail. Dove, as the newspaper described him, "had resided in Frankfort for some time, was a peaceable, law abiding citizen, who had a wife and six children, and from the appearance of his home, no one would suspect his having any

Headline in the *Ilion Citizen*, December 12, 1907.

great amount of money." The article continued: "It seems that Frankfort is cursed with an unusually large number of dangerous law defying citizens.… According to Chief Getman these black hand threats have been going on for the past year.…The situation is a grave one and the officials of Frankfort should use every measure possible to stamp out the conditions existing."

From the 1930s to the 1960s, disappearances and other crimes, especially illegal gambling, took place in the two towns. Crime in Herkimer and Frankfort began to fade throughout the 1970s and 1980s. Eventually, organized crime fully ceased in the area, marking the end of the area's history with the Mafia.

15

GRACE UNDER PRESSURE

BY ROBERTA WALSH

For fifteen years in the 1940s and '50s, the Lilac Rest Nursing Home on West Street in Newport, New York, was owned and operated by Grace Haley Parks. A few elderly residents who could afford a private nursing home occupied small but tidy rooms and enjoyed home-cooked meals. Parks was said to run a tight ship. What her clients didn't know was that she was a jailbird. That's right. Grace Parks had spent some time in the hoosegow.

Grace Haley was born in 1903 in Forestport, New York. When the family moved to Newport, her father, Martin Haley, worked as a fireman at Newport Cotton Manufacturing Company. He had married Rose Grace Boyce in 1894, and daughter Grace was the third of their twelve children. Grace attended school until the seventh grade. By age sixteen, she was punching a time clock and collecting a paycheck as a machine operator in the cotton mill. Since she was earning money, she may have felt that she had also earned some independence. But parents and teenagers don't always agree on the boundaries.

In 1865, a law was passed in New York called the Disorderly Child Act (chap. 172, § 5, 1865 N.Y. Laws 293). If a parent or guardian complained that a child was disorderly, a warrant could be issued for the child's arrest, and the child could be taken into police custody. All the parent had to do was lodge a complaint; it wasn't necessary for the child to have committed a crime. Often, the child had run away from home, had been talking "sass" or had been associating with friends the parents didn't approve of.

So, it came to pass in July 1920 in Newport, New York, that Martin Haley got fed right up with his seventeen-year-old daughter, Grace. He had had just about all the sass he was prepared to take. That's when he called on the police and lodged a complaint against her. Grace was arraigned before Justice Walker in Newport and charged with being a "disorderly child." Martin was there to say that Grace wouldn't do as she was told. Walker sent Grace to the Herkimer County jail.

Grace sat in her cell for some days while attorney Donald L. Brush requested an appeal. On August 3, Grace appeared before County Judge Charles Bell, who granted her appeal based on the fact that the Disorderly Child Act of 1865 had been changed in 1886! In 1920, parents could no longer send their children to jail without cause. Grace had been arrested and sent to jail under a New York State law that hadn't been on the books for almost thirty-five years!

16
WILD, WILD BEAVER RIVER

BY PEG MASTERS, TOWN OF WEBB HISTORIAN

In early October 1923, a liquor-crazed lumberjack known as "Tennessee" went to his cabin after a fistfight with another lumberjack at the Beaver River Hotel and retrieved a .45-caliber automatic revolver. Tennessee began terrorizing the hamlet by firing shots into the hotel. Across the street, William Brown was outside Maude Lang's boardinghouse stacking wood. Tennessee's next shot missed Brown but seared a lock of hair off Maude's right temple. The rampage continued as bullets were fired at several other lumberjacks along the roadway. State troopers from Old Forge eventually got to Beaver River and took Tennessee into custody.

Beaver River Station is situated on six-tenths of a square mile of land on the east end of the Stillwater Reservoir in the town of Webb in northern Herkimer County. It is completely surrounded by the Adirondack Park with no road access. In 1923, passenger and freight trains were the primary link to the outside world. For decades, sportsmen were attracted to this remote region. Accommodations were limited to a few lodges established by their Adirondack guides. Bert B. Bullock began advertising his Norridgewock House in 1899 with rooms available for seven to ten dollars per week. After his lodge burned in May 1914, B.B. began selling off adjacent parcels for private seasonal camps. Generators or kerosene provided power for lights, propane was used for refrigerators and stoves and wood stoves heated the

Beaver River Hotel. *Courtesy of the Town of Webb Historical Association, Old Forge, New York.*

camps in cold weather, which often saw temperatures drop to thirty degrees below zero during the winter.

In June 1923, the newly formed Black River Regulating District (BRRD), pressured by mill owners on the Black River below the Stillwater Dam, got word that Governor Alfred E. Smith had signed the "Williams Bill" to clear-cut nearly four thousand acres of "forever wild" forestlands along the reservoir. The Stillwater Dam on the western edge of the reservoir was going to be raised by nineteen feet. Some private camps on land in Stillwater and at Beaver River Station were purchased by BRRD and demolished or had to be moved above the anticipated high waterline by their owners where possible.

Hundreds of lumberjacks descended on the area to clear-cut the shoreline along the flow. Most of the men were packed into shacks or tent camps, with only the ground to sleep on that winter. Reports soon reached the outside world that liquor was flowing freely in the camps, violating the Volstead Act prohibiting the manufacture and sale of alcohol.

A Prohibition squadron from Utica conducted a raid at Beaver River in October 1923. Its mission was to track down a rumor that most of the illegal booze was being served at Harry Smith's café and at a hotel conducted by Charles Ellerby. The agents secured evidence against Smith and Ellerby and placed them under arrest. Smith's wife, Jessie, was alleged to have assisted her husband with supplying liquor to the lumberjacks. "Wild Jess" was known far and wide as the "Queen" of the camps, fearlessly riding through the hamlet on her pony with a six-shooter on her side. The squadron decided not to challenge Jessie's participation in selling booze or ask if she carried a permit for her gun.

A number of the lumberjacks were also packing firearms. Not long after the raid, Maude Lang's daughter, Mary, and her woodsman fiancé stepped off the midnight train at Beaver River to a welcoming party of dozens of lumberjacks firing shotguns and pistols into the air. The couple had gone to Tupper Lake expecting to be married, but Mary was not a resident of Franklin County and was denied a marriage license. Armed troopers guarding prisoners on the train from Dannemora leapt from the train with their pistols drawn, expecting a shootout, only to find it was an impromptu celebration for the bride and groom.

Reports of the stabbing death of a Polish lumberjack in one of the camps brought state troopers back to Beaver River in May 1924. The free-for-all fight began about noon and lasted until after midnight. Several dozen woodsmen, described as foreigners, were stabbed with knives and pommeled over the head with bottles. No arrests were made, but the troopers continued to search the woods for eyewitnesses to the brawl.

A week later, on May 12, 1924, state troopers were summoned to investigate a fire at Beaver River that leveled a hotel owned by George Vincent. About twenty lumberjacks were asleep on the second floor and narrowly escaped the inferno by climbing down ladders hoisted to their bedroom windows. George was trapped in a room on the first floor and was burned to death beyond recognition, along with his housekeeper, Mary Des Chambeau, who was found four feet from the outside door. Her husband, Amos, worked in one of the camps nearby.

The state was determined to stop the wholesale lawlessness at Beaver River, which was fueled by liquor. Passengers who got off the train at the station had their luggage searched by state troopers. Whether you were a man or a woman, your packages were shredded and your clothing scattered about the platform. One day, troopers managed to confiscate six gallons of illegal booze stored in maple syrup cans. A former lumberjack was later arrested when he admitted to carrying liquor in a package. This surprised his wife, who thought he was working as a traveling salesman in the city. A complaint was filed by a conductor on behalf of the distraught train passengers, who felt humiliated and were threatened with arrest if they did not cooperate.

Wild Jessie Smith met every train and reportedly enjoyed the alleged holdups of the passengers. She knew that most of the illegal beverages came from stills deep in the woods. Charles Ellerby brewed beer in Big Moose. He paid local kids a quarter or a half-dollar a day to wash bottles and cinch down the caps with a special spring-loaded lever device.

Forest fires due to dry conditions that fall prompted the state to shut down all hunting and camping in the Adirondacks. But the lumberjacks and dam workers had completed their work ahead of schedule. On February, 11, 1925, the gates on the enlarged dam at Stillwater were closed and then opened for the first release of water on May 6. The state conservation commission authorized the planting of twenty-five thousand trees along the ravaged perimeter of the reservoir.

Nearly a century later, the reservoir offers a multitude of recreational possibilities, including remote wilderness camping, canoeing, boating, fishing, hunting and snowmobiling. There are about one hundred seasonal camps at Beaver River, which still has no road access or electrical services. "It is ironic because the Reservoir we are abutting was dammed with the express purpose of using the water for power. It all goes southwest of us," noted the late Pat Thompson in her 2000 memoir of her life at Beaver River as a co-proprietor with her husband, Stanley, of the Norridgewock Lodge for five decades.

The Norridgewock has been rebuilt several times after devastating fires but remains the heart of the community. Thompson family members have operated it for several generations and are among the fewer than ten

Hotel picture at Beaver River. *Courtesy of Town of Webb Historical Association, Old Forge, New York.*

full-time, year-round residents of the hamlet. Guests, day-trippers and all essential supplies—food, propane, building materials, household goods and even cars—are brought in on water taxis and barges from the boat launch at Stillwater on the western end of the reservoir.

It is hard to imagine today the wild chaos that surrounded Beaver River in 1923–24 while sipping a legal beverage, gazing out over the pristine landscape, listening to the call of the loons or enjoying the tranquility of a beautiful sunset. Articles about Wild Jess surface now and then. Locals do pay some homage to their defiant history and ignore motor vehicle registration laws by driving around Beaver River's dusty roads in their rusty cars and other vehicles without license plates. New York officials apparently have more wicked things to investigate.

17

HE SHOT HER IN THE CORSET

by Diane Fagan Affleck

"He shot her in the corset." That's how family lore always described the brutal attack on Cora Morey Helmer by the hired man. The *Utica Saturday Globe* devoted more than half of a page and seven photographs to the "Deed of a Fiend."[23]

William Brayton was a twenty-three-year-old farmhand working for Devillo Helmer (1858–1944) and Cora Morey Helmer (1862–1932) on their farm in Kast Bridge, New York, three miles north of Herkimer. According to the *Globe*, Brayton had worked for the Helmers for several years, and Devillo had dismissed Will, as he was called, more than once. Each time, Brayton pleaded for his job and told Helmer that "he looked upon Mr. and Mrs. Helmer with reverence akin to what he would feel for his own parents." Every time, Devillo had relented—until April 1915, when Brayton learned that there would be no reprieve. Interestingly, Devillo's cousin Nancy Helmer Folts, who lived close by, wrote in her diary simply that Will's term of service had expired.[24] Whatever the case, it appears that Brayton felt aggrieved, and as the *Globe* tells it, he brooded about his unfortunate situation and blamed Cora for his dismissal.

The newspaper may have been right about that. The *Globe* article claims that Brayton had made neighbors so uncomfortable that they advised Devillo and Cora to let the young man go. In response, Devillo had laughed and said, "Will wouldn't hurt a fly!" Worse yet, according to the paper, some people said Brayton had gone about the neighborhood at night, peeking

Above: Devillo and Cora Morey Helmer's farm at Kast Bridge, New York, from the *Utica Saturday Globe* (April 10, 1915).

Right: Cora Morey Helmer, from the *Utica Saturday Globe* (April 10, 1915).

The Helmer parlor, "Where Mrs. Helmer Fought for Life and Honor," according to the *Utica Saturday Globe* (April 10, 1915).

into people's windows. Still, Devillo always kept him on because Will was a "good and faithful workman." Devillo didn't want to "to let him go because of women's whims."[25] Perhaps Devillo should have paid more attention to Cora and the neighbors.

Late on a cloudy Tuesday afternoon, April 6, 1915, Brayton decided to take action. He went to the house while Devillo was at work in the barn, "threw his arms around [Cora] and struggled to fling her to the floor." She resisted and screamed for help but could not be heard in the barn. Brayton, "thwarted in the base designs he first carried in his mind," then pulled a revolver from his pocket and shot her at very close range in her side. As she "sank to the floor and the pool of blood flowed deeper and wider near her prostrate form," Brayton fled.[26]

When Devillo found his wife injured and lying on the floor, he ran to the Kast Bridge Hotel, where Melvin Uhlinger called the authorities. Sheriff William Stitt, a deputy, the coroner and Dr. Cyrus Kay all hurried to Kast Bridge by automobile to help Cora Helmer and pursue the would-be assassin. Following the direction Brayton had been seen to go, the sheriff

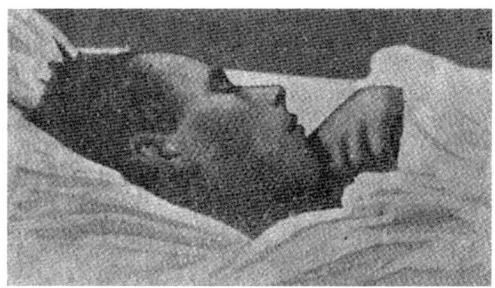

William Brayton lying in his hospital bed, from the *Utica Saturday Globe* (April 10, 1915).

and Uhlinger chased after him. Pretty quickly, "the scent grew hot" as Brayton came out of a ravine and into view. The sheriff ordered the young man to stand still or he would shoot. In fact, the sheriff had given his gun to Uhlinger and was unarmed, but Brayton fell for the bluff and surrendered. But as he walked toward the sheriff, Brayton pulled out his gun and shot himself in the side.[27] Within the hour, both Cora and Will were patients in the Herkimer Emergency Hospital on North Washington Street in the village, occupying rooms across the hall from each other. They were both seriously injured, and we know from Nancy Helmer Folts's diary that Cora remained in the hospital until May 3, when she finally went home with a "'trained nurse' to care for her."[28]

One aspect of the story not reported in the *Globe* is that Brayton fled into the sugarbush, the woods up the hill and behind the Lester Helmer homestead at Kast Bridge. Up in the woods, he ran into Howard Helmer (1899–1975) at the sugar hut, where the teenager was processing the spring run of sap. According to the family story, Brayton's eyes were absolutely wild. But fortunately for all of us who came after, Will did not hurt Howard other than scaring him a bit.

In July 1915, Will Brayton was convicted of second-degree attempted murder and sentenced to Auburn State Prison for a term of from twelve to twenty-four years.[29] Cora Helmer lived for another seventeen years and died in 1932 at the age of seventy. This has long been a well-known incident in my family, always referred to as the time "he shot her in the corset." Unfortunately, I don't know who described it that way first, but the description passed into family lore.

Devillo Helmer is my first cousin three times removed—at least I think that's right. His grandfather is my great-great-great-grandfather (Philip P. Helmer–> Matthew Helmer, brother of Luther–> William Helmer–> Devillo Helmer married Cora Morey) and (Philip P. Helmer–> Luther Helmer, brother of Matthew–> Nancy Helmer Folts–> Rosabel Folts Helmer–> Howard P. Helmer–> Madeline Helmer Fagan–> me). Devillo and Cora's home still stands in Kast Bridge.

18
DON'T ASK ANY QUESTIONS

by Susan R. Perkins

I asked my Uncle Harry Perkins what he knew about great-uncle Leigh Jay Perkins (1890–1965). His response was that his mother told him, "Don't ask any questions when Uncle Leigh comes to visit." Apparently, every time he came to visit, he would have a different woman with him. We all have someone in our family tree who was a real character, and my Uncle Leigh was ours. He was married six times and divorced five times, and one of the marriages was annulled. As a matter of fact, he was married to two women at the same time.

Leigh's first wife was Gertrude "Gertie" Eleanor Kibbie, whom he married on December 26, 1906, at the Methodist Episcopal Church in Dolgeville. His second wife was widow Emma Wiley Crossman; they married on May 31, 1917. Emma's previous husband, Ralph Crossman, had been the proprietor of the American Hotel until his death in 1914. Leigh became the manager of the American Hotel when Emma was the proprietor, and that is how they made their acquaintance and eventually married. There was just one problem, unbeknownst to Emma: Leigh was still married to Gertrude Kibbie.

In November 1916, Leigh stated that he and Gertie were divorced and that she had procured the divorce in Paris, Illinois. When questioned, Gertie denied that she had ever been to Illinois. But she was soon to rectify that situation. On June 11, 1917, there was a trial in the State Supreme Court in Herkimer County for an action for divorce— plaintiff Gertie Kibbie Perkins

Left: Leigh Perkins and Gertrude Kibbie. *Editors' collection*.

Below: The American Hotel, located on the corner of North Helmer Avenue and West State Street in Dolgeville. *Editors' collection*.

versus Leigh J. Perkins, defendant. The court ruled that the defendant had committed adultery with Emma Crossman and ever since had been living in an adulterous relationship with her at the American Hotel in the village of Dolgeville. On November 12, 1917, the court stated: "That it shall be lawful for the said Gertie Kibbie Perkins, the plaintiff, to resume her maiden name of Gertie Kibbie, and to marry again in the same manner as if the said Leigh J. Perkins the defendant was actually dead; but it shall not be lawful for the said Leigh J. Perkins, the defendant, to marry any other person until the said plaintiff shall be actually dead."

Now it was Emma's turn. On November 6, 1918, Leigh was living in Youngstown, Ohio, when he was served a summons and complaint by Emma Crossman of Dolgeville. During the trial, it was stated that Gertie and Leigh last lived as husband and wife in 1913 and Leigh had stated to Emma that Gertie filed for divorce in Illinois, which now everyone knew never happened. On May 5, 1919, the marriage with Emma Crossman Perkins was annulled.

But time heals all wounds. Life moves on. Maybe a little thing like a court decree does, too—or, in truth, Leigh's agreement to it had. He ignored the order that he wasn't to marry until Gertie Kibbie was dead. On July 13, 1920, in Syracuse, New York, he married his third wife, Clara M. Lawson. The marriage certificate stated that he was living in Youngstown, Ohio, and that Clara was living in Utica, New York. They managed to live together exactly nine years to the date. They divorced on July 13, 1929, in Flint, Michigan. Extreme cruelty was the reason for the divorce. The alimony was one dollar.

Days later, on July 22, Leigh married his fourth wife, Eunice Whittaker Scofield, in Flint. They both stated that they had been married once before. Her previous husband was Harry Schofield, and they had a son, Harry Jr. The marriage of Leigh and Eunice lasted five years; the couple divorced on December 22, 1934, in Flint. Extreme cruelty was the reason for the divorce. The alimony was fifty dollars.

On May 13, 1936, Leigh married his fifth wife, Rachel Hamilton, and he was still living in Flint. This marriage may have lasted the longest, as the couple stayed together for fourteen years. They divorced on January 3, 1951. But Leigh may have met his match with Rachel. She had been divorced two times before she married Leigh, and she married three more times after their divorce.

That may not have been Leigh's last marriage. The sixth time may have been the charm. According to the Flint, Michigan City Directory of 1952,

Leigh is listed with a wife by the name of Ruth, who was a salesperson at a dress shop. I wasn't able to find a marriage record for them.

While I was working at the Herkimer County Historical Society, a couple came in doing research, and we started talking. They said they were going to Gracelawn Cemetery in Flint, Michigan. I proceeded to tell them about great-uncle Leigh and that he was buried in that same cemetery. They offered to take a picture of the gravestone. They did so and emailed it to me.

My parents went to visit great-uncle Leigh on their honeymoon. Thank goodness they had a marriage that lasted thirty-five years. My Aunt Helen Perkins Schultz told me once that Leigh married and divorced Rachel twice—that would make seven wives. I have no proof of it. Henry the VIII had six wives; well, great-uncle Leigh may have him beat by one.

19

THE MURDER OF WINIFRED GETMAN

by Susan Perkins

The victim was Winifred Leonard Getman (1897–1916), the daughter of John and Catherine (Stark) Leonard of Little Falls. She married Ralph Getman (1896–1958) on June 15, 1915. Ralph was the son of William and Harriet (Osterhaut) Getman of Ilion.

Ralph and Winifred Getman had been married just a short time and had an eight-month-old son, Francis Joseph Getman (1915–1958), when the couple became estranged. On May 30, 1916, Ralph went to Little Falls to the Globe Hotel, where Winifred was living with her mother and their son. Winifred's uncle George Stark was operating the hotel on West John Street. Knowing he would be barred from entering the hotel, Ralph climbed onto the roof and went through a window to Winifred's room, where he found her with their son. He threatened her with a .38-caliber revolver and told her to be quiet or he would shoot. He took their son from her arms and went back out the window. He went to Ilion, where he was apprehended by the police. The baby was taken back to his mother.

A month later, on July 8, Winifred had taken the trolley to Utica to a park. Returning home, at a stop in Ilion, Ralph happened to see her on the trolley and jumped on board to confront her. An argument ensued. They both took the trolley to Little Falls and were spotted by her mother walking along the tracks, quarrelling. Mrs. Leonard convinced them to come back to the Globe Hotel. Ralph still carried a revolver with him. George Stark came in and told Ralph that the police were coming to arrest him for stealing the revolver from Daniel Nast's pawnshop in Little Falls. Hearing that, Ralph pulled out the gun and shot three times. The first shot was aimed at George Stark and missed. The second shot went through a window. The final shot was aimed at Winifred. As Ralph pointed the gun at her, he said, "Winnie, I am going to shoot you—Kiss me for the last time." She was seated in a rocking chair, holding baby Francis. The shot rang out. The baby fell to the floor, uninjured. Winifred had been hit in the left lung. It would prove to be a mortal wound several days later.

Ralph made a hasty escape after committing his dastardly deed and for a while was living on the run out west under the alias Charles Moyer. His life after that day came to light when he wrote his mother in 1920 from prison in Tucker, Arkansas, being held there for forgery. He had been trapping in the Midwest, placer gold mining in Mexico and sailing with a steamship line up and down the Pacific Coast. In the letter, he told his mother, "My heart is heavy as lead. I am confined in a prison here for a two-year term for stealing, which act I did because I was starving." He told his mother to tell the Herkimer County sheriff where he was. In the meantime, witnesses to the shooting died, including Winifred's mother, Catherine; her uncle George Stark; and the coroner, Dr. Ward E. Hunt.

After Getman served out his sentence in Arkansas, District Attorney George Ward and Herkimer County sheriff George Firth went to Arkansas to bring him back to Herkimer County to be tried for murder in 1922. While he was held in the Herkimer County Jail, Ralph's sister Blanche Getman Monohan brought a very special visitor to see him. It was his son, Francis, just seven years old, who was told that the man he was meeting was "Uncle Ralph." Getman was tried and convicted of murder in the second degree and sentenced to Auburn State Prison on July 12, 1922, for a term of twenty years to life. He gained his freedom in 1933, when New York governor Herbert Lehman commuted his sentence in time for Christmas. He was given a new suit of clothes, a twenty-dollar bill and transportation to a city in New York where he was given employment. But where did Ralph end up after that? The only information that could be found was a listing of a Ralph Getman, correct age, in the 1940 census as an inmate at Attica State Prison. At the same time the census was taken in April, his mother, Harriet, had died. Her obituary stated that Ralph was living in Los Angeles, California. Was the family embarrassed to list the real location of the wayward son? Also found on Ancestry.com was a 1942 World War II draft registration card for Ralph Parker Getman, living in Warsaw, New York, which is the Wyoming County seat. It is just thirteen miles from Attica State Prison. Ralph died in 1958 in Chicago, Illinois.

1934 Ilion High School Football team high school yearbook photo. Francis Monohan is seen in this photo in the third row, far right. The identification of the entire team is as follows: *from left to right, front row*: F. Serow, J. Morris, M. Goldin, E. Manion, L. Luther, J. Caswell, J. Dare, L. Waters; *second row*: A. Barnum, J. Manion, S. Welch, F. Campbell; *third row*: J. Bowers, A. Rathbun, K. France, L. Edwards, F. Monahan; *fourth row*: E. Morris, J. McAllister, P. Kinney, M. Williams, E. Snow, T. Leonard, F. Harter; *fifth row*: M. Rasbach, J. Mackin, V. Connors, K. Goering, H. Hendrix, K. Bleau; *sixth row*: J. Fitzer, G. Trimble, Coach Bemis, R. Currier, I. France, B. Smith, A. Pelletier. *Courtesy of Ilion Free Library*.

What happened to baby Francis? He was taken in by his paternal grandmother, Harriet Getman (1861–1940), and then by his aunt Blanche Getman Monohan (1890–1966), who adopted her nephew and gave him the last name Monohan. They first lived in Winnipeg, Canada, but by 1918, the family was in Minneapolis, Minnesota. In 1920, they were living in Indianapolis, Indiana. They returned to Herkimer County in time for the 1930 census, where we see them living in Ilion, where Francis graduated from high school in 1936. He was a tabulating-machine service manager for Remington Rand for twelve years, including six years in Albany. He married Erna Follmer on July 4, 1939, in Little Falls, New York. They had three sons, Terry, Jon and Richard, and lived in Clifton Heights. In 1950, Francis died at the young age of thirty-five. As he was driving home from work on Washington Avenue in Albany, a tree crashed across his car in a terrible windstorm. He is buried in Armory Hill Cemetery in Ilion.

I was happy to find that Francis led a happy life. Newspaper articles on his death conveyed the sense that he was a wonderful husband and a devoted father.

20
TRIAL TO TRIUMPH

An Immigrant Family's Story

BY PATRICIA MASI STOCK, LITTLE FALLS CITY HISTORIAN

This story reflects the life of an Italian immigrant family that made a new life in this country. It also tells the tale of what happens when, after trying to accost a woman's young daughter, you taunt the woman that she will not dare shoot you with the gun she has aimed at you.

Monteleone di Puglia is a hill town in the province of Foggia. It is a beautiful area surrounded by millions of legally protected olive trees in southeastern Italy. It was first settled by traveling Greeks and at the beginning of the twentieth century had three dialects close to that language, as well as a Puglia dialect. This is where Salvatricia Palma was born to Antonio and Maria Visconti Palma on April 7, 1890. The climate there is mild, ranging from forty to eighty degrees Fahrenheit—much different from central New York, where Salvatricia would live out her life, as employment was readily found in Little Falls mills.

Also born in Monteleone was Leonard Anthony Lavista, on a spring morning, April 1, 1882. His parents, Rocco and Lucy, came to Little Falls in 1896, bringing Leonard with them. They lived at 311 Third Street. Leonard, or Tony, as he was sometimes known, returned to Italy and married Salvatricia on August 7, 1907. He stayed in Italy with his growing family but then returned to Little Falls to work in the Barnett Tannery. He had become an American citizen in 1903.

Salvatricia traveled to the American embassy in Rome from her home in 1917 to apply for an emergency passport. She was expecting their fourth child, Angelina, who would be born in Little Falls in October 1917.

Mrs. Salvatricia "Salvi" Lavista arrived in Little Falls, where the family set up house at 12 North Second Street. She found work at the Phoenix Mill. She had brought the three children born in Italy with her—Rocco Anthony, born in 1908; Lucia "Lucy," born in 1910; and Dorthea, born in 1912. The three children attended school in Little Falls.

Carmello Tamberro had lived in the Lavista house with his wife before the Lavistas moved in. The Tamberro couple visited the Lavistas soon after they had moved in, looking for a quilt they might have left behind. They were again at the Lavista house for a funeral when a Lavista baby died.

Lucy came home early from school one day because she was sick. Carmello Tamberro came by her house and offered her a penny. She said she did not want it and to give it to her little sister. Tamberro instead supposedly grabbed her arm and took her partway down the cellar stairs. Her older brother, Rocco, was home and told Tamberro to stop what he was doing or he would call the police. Tamberro was at first hesitant but let Lucy go, and both came up the stairs. Tamberro left, but not before threatening to come back on Monday.

When Lucy told her mother what had happened, Salvi told her daughter to not tell her father, because she did not think Tamberro meant any harm. Salvi, though, warned her daughter that, in the future, if she was home alone, she should lock the door and not let anyone into the house.

According to testimony, on March 10, 1920, Carmello Tamberro, a city employee, was working on a catch basin at the intersection of Albany and Second Streets. Lucy was at home for two months from school due to illness. Her brother, Rocco, and her sister Dorthea were at school. Lucy, no doubt, saw Tamberro when she went to the store for her mother. She was supposed to get cloth but instead came home with a fashion sheet. Her mother was home with a two-month-old daughter, Mary Lucy, because whooping cough was going around the company's nursery. Salvi was washing dishes in the kitchen when Lucy called out to her from the front room. Almost immediately, Tamberro came to the kitchen door and began talking to Salvi. She accused him of trying to make improper advances toward her daughter. Salvi attempted to get by him, but he grabbed her and tried to force her back into the kitchen. She broke away from him, yelled to her daughter to get the gun from upstairs and proceeded to the dining room of the house. Salvi had the gun pointed at him. Tamberro had an ice pick in his hand, threatening her. He told her: "I am forty-four years old. You would not shoot me." Salvi and Tamberro struggled for the gun. The gun went off, according to Salvi's testimony, and Tamberro was shot.

Tamberro left the house and slowly walked up Second Street. He was helped by a Mr. Foote to Dr. Eberle's office around 1:30 p.m. When Harry Steele came by with his horse-drawn sleigh, the wounded man was subsequently taken to the hospital, where he gave a statement. Tamberro explained that he was working and just went to the Lavista house to ask for a drink of water. The bullet had entered his right chest, gone through a lung and lodged in the back muscles. At 11:00 p.m., it was suspected he might not live.

District Attorney Ward was just returning to his office on Main and Second Streets and heard the shot. He called the police. Soon after, Captain Dunden and Officer McLaughlin arrived at the house. Salvi told them what had happened and where the gun was, and she indicated the bullet in the floor. They searched and found a Colt revolver .38 and an ice hook, which she referred to as a stiletto, as well as a spent shell. She and Lucy were taken to the DA's office, but not before Lucy ran to the tannery to get her father.

Leonard Lavista was questioned about Tamberro. Leonard said that Tamberro had been at his house twice that he knew, once looking for the quilt and once when attending his child's funeral. They were not on very good terms. Tamberro, it turned out, was his cousin and lived on Flint Avenue (formerly German Street) above a bakery. He knew Tamberro was married and had a twenty-year-old son.

Salvi and Lucy, at the DA's office, explained what had happened. Lucy added that she was in the second grade at St. Mary's Academy and that Tamberro had been to the house on February 7 and on Wednesday. Sheriff Cress arrived around 6:00 p.m., charged Salvi with assault in the first degree and took her to the Herkimer County Jail. She was described as a woman in her thirties with black hair and a small build. When Tamberro died on the morning of March 12, the charge was changed to manslaughter, first degree.

Carmelo Tamberro's funeral was held on March 15, 1920. His body had been taken to Dineen's funeral home and then to his home on Flint Avenue. The funeral ceremony was held at St. Mary's Church, and his countrymen made it an elaborate affair. He was buried in the Old St. Mary's Cemetery in Little Falls.

Salvi was in jail for a week. Her bail was set at $6,000. Three good friends of the family helped with the bail money. They were Antonio Lamanna, Tony Morra and Luciano Scarano.

Salvi stayed home with her family, who was very happy to have her until the start of the trial. The trial was postponed when a physician filed an affidavit that she was in ill health.

An all-male jury was chosen, despite women recently gaining the right to vote. The jurors were William Petrie, George H. Sprague, Herbert Toma, Fred House and Herbert W. Batchelor from Herkimer; Fred March and Robert Milton from Salisbury; Harren R. Knapp from IIion; John W. Nort from Dolgeville; James J. Blauvelt from Poland; Raymond A. Denton from Frankfort; and John Burke from Litchfield. Notably, none were from Little Falls.

At the trial, which began in March 1922, Salvi brought her two-month-old son and one-year-old Mary Lucy, along with many friends and her husband. She was described as a small woman about forty years of age. There were few witnesses. Two for the defense were Florence DelGrand and Asunta Vidodula. Originally, former county judge Robert F. Livingston was to be defense council, but Charles B. Hane joined him. Florence was asked what she had seen on March 10, 1920. Florence said she knew both families involved. She said she saw Tamberro go into the house and Lucy come out on the step and look up and down the street. Later, she saw Tamberro come out the door and go up the street. Asunta said she saw something about two weeks before and knew only the Lavista family and could see their front door from her home. She saw Tamberro on the street blowing a kiss at Lucy, who was standing in the window. Then she saw him go into the house, saw Lucy come out and go back in, then saw Tamberro come out. She did not know in what direction he had gone.

The prosecution took the testimony of these witnesses rather than the grand jury statements of June 1920, which differed somewhat. At that time, a Beatrice Morando from Binghamton, speaking for the prosecution, had told the court that the defendant told her that she did not think Tamberro had any evil designs on the daughter. And Charles Baly, as interpreter for Salvi, said she told him she went behind a mirror in the dining room to obtain the gun. But the interpreter also pointed out that the dialect in which she spoke confused some pronouns, making it difficult to ascertain who she was talking about.

It was noted that there was a city tool house close to Second Street and that city employees went there in the morning and at noon for drinking water.

It was also stated in a Richfield Springs newspaper, "The participants are of the better class of Italians and much sympathy is expressed for Mrs. Lavista."

Salvi stood rather emotionless, as she had been during the trial, when the verdict was read. She was acquitted and was released to go home.

By the 1930 census, the family was living on Loomis Street. Another child, a boy, Maurice Peck, had joined the family in 1923. A son-in-law, Napoleon Morra, Lucy's husband, now lived with them. The Lavistas had nine children born between the years 1908 and 1933. They had lost only the one child as an infant. After the trial, the family went on living their lives, contributing to the economy and the culture of the valley and the nation.

The oldest son, Rocco, lived with his parents until he married Bessie DeLorenzo on January 12, 1935. Mr. and Mrs. Sam DePiazza were best man and matron of honor. Sam Zambri was an usher. They then moved to Burwell Street until they bought a duplex on Loomis Street. Rocco served in the U.S. Navy in World War II. He owned a taxi service in Little Falls. He was involved in youth baseball after the family moved to Gloversville in 1951. The couple had two children, Daniel J. Lavista and Sylvia Lavista.

Daniel graduated from Gloversville High School, where he was an outstanding athlete. He went on to Siena College and the University of Dayton. He began a teaching career at Tilton School in New Hampshire. Daniel married Rosemary Broderick in 1968 and soon after became an assistant professor of English at the Community College of the Finger Lakes. Later, he was president of College of the Lake Country and became chancellor for Los Angeles Community College District, the nation's largest community college. Daniel retired in 2013 to pursue other professional interests and family affairs. Daniel and his wife have two grown children and now live in Charleston, South Carolina.

Rocco and Bessie's daughter, Sylvia, also went to Gloversville High School and attended Empire Girls State. She was an accomplished tennis player. Before she married, she worked as an engineer's assistant at GE in Schenectady. Later, she was a textile artist. Sylvia married Joseph Persico, who had gone to SUNY Albany and Columbia University. He served in the military during the Korean War. He then worked for the U.S. Information Office and was stationed with his wife at the embassy in Rio de Janeiro, Brazil, and the U.S. embassy in Argentina. Their first daughter, Vanya Maria, was born in Buenos Aires, Argentina, in 1960. The family then moved back to the United States, where Joseph worked for Governors Harriman, Rockefeller and Wilson and the state health department. They lived in Guilderland, and their second daughter was born in Albany in 1963. Joseph became a writer of history and was a close friend of Secretary of State Colin Powell. He was asked to write a quote for the World War II Memorial. He wrote, "Here we mark the price of freedom." Joseph Persico died in 2014, and Sylvia Persico died in 2018. They are buried in Saratoga National Cemetery.

Lucy married Napoleon Morra on Valentine's Day in 1927. She had gone to high school for one year and then worked in a dress factory. At first, the couple lived with her parents, then they moved to East Monroe Street. Her husband was a tailor by trade. They were living in Dolgeville by 1940, and Napoleon had his own tailor shop. They had two sons, Pasquale "Patsy" and Anthony Morra. Patsy was the ring bearer in Uncle Rocco's wedding. The two young men became interested in dentistry. Patsy went to school at Hartwick College, New York, and then attended Georgetown Dental School in Washington, D.C., for orthodontics. He married Theresa Tripodi and opened an office in Dolgeville. The couple had two sons, Joseph and Marcus. A huge fire in Dolgeville destroyed the Opera Block in 1962; by 1970, Dr. Morra had moved his practice to Rockville, Maryland.

Anthony went into the army and rose to the rank of captain. He became a dental surgeon and married Angelina D'Arcangelis. He first practiced in Washington, D.C., then opened an office in Latham in 1958. Their first son, Antonio L., was born in Washington. A second son, Gregory, continues the dental practice. Anthony and Angelina had a third son, Daniel, and a daughter, Valerie. They have ten grandchildren and five great-grandchildren.

Dorthea was the last child to be born in Italy to Salvi and Leonard. She was five when she came to the United States. After leaving school, she worked for a time at Melrose Slipper in Little Falls. She married Alfred Weaver in May 1935. Her wedding shower was at the Sons of Italy Hall, of which her father was a charter member. It later became the DeCarlo-Staffo Post Home. They lived at 218 Loomis Street and had a son, Wilford, on January 10, 1940. Wilford later worked at the shoe factory. Dorthea was in Long Beach, California, by 1966. Her son died in June 1983.

Angelina was the fourth child of Leonard and Salvi Lavista. She was the child Salvi was carrying when she immigrated to the United States. Angelina married Joseph DeLorenzo and moved to Campbell, Pennsylvania. They also lived in Binghamton, and Joseph spent thirty-plus years in the shoe industry. Two children were born of this union, Marie and Phillip. Angelina died in January 2010 in Gainesville, Prince William County, Virginia.

Mary Lucy was the child at her mother's side at the trial. She was a year old at the time. Mary had a beauty parlor in Little Falls, and her husband, Joseph Candello, had a billiards hall for a time. By 1992, they were living in Dolgeville. They had two daughters: Kathleen, who married Charles Provorse; and Lorraine, who served as the librarian of the Dolgeville Public

Manheim Library until retirement due to illness. She died in 2005. Her father died in 2006; her mother had died in 1997.

Blaise P. was the infant whose hunger cries interrupted the trial. He grew up in Little Falls but left to work in West Hempstead, New York. He married Frances Lallones in 1948. They were living in Long Beach, California, in 1965. He worked as a salesman. He died in West Hempstead in January 2011.

Maurice Peck was born in late summer 1923. He worked in West Hampton Beach in 1966 and later moved to Melbourne, Florida. He died in November 2011.

The last of the Lavista family, Leonard Anthony Jr., was born during the depths of the Depression, in 1933. He married Gilda Florentino from Herkimer in Detroit, Michigan, in St. Aloysius Church in 1952. They returned to Herkimer and lived with her parents for a while. He was employed as a shoe worker and later for the railroad. By 1959, they had moved to Palm Bay, Florida. Their children grew up there. Their first daughter was Deborah, who married George Keesee of Merrit Island in Rockledge, Florida. Their son was Leonard Anthony Lavista III. He married Cynthia Ann Freix in 1981. Diana Lavista, a second daughter, was also born to this union. The couple divorced in 1971.

Salvi Lavista and her husband attended St. Joseph's Church in Dolgeville. She lived to see much of the growth of her family. She passed away in 1966 and is buried in St. Joseph's Cemetery in Dolgeville. Her husband had worked for the railroad for thirty-seven years. In 1949, he retired and worked for Dr. Bergin as a gardener. He passed away in 1974 in Eden Park Nursing Home in Cobleskill and is buried beside his wife.

21

THE GILLETTE CELL

BY JAMES GREINER

On July 14, 1906, Chester Gillette arrived in Herkimer and was immediately brought to the county jail. By now, he was front-page news as the murderer of Grace Brown. As he descended the stairs to the basement of the jail, one had to wonder if Chester by chance looked over his shoulder to catch a glimpse of the courthouse where his fate would be decided. Once inside the limestone jail, he was led to the first room on the right, the administrative or booking office. Here, his name and other details about him were recorded in a ledger. When the paperwork was completed, a deputy brought him to one of the cells in the basement. This arrangement didn't last long. Due to the immense press coverage Chester had received, scores of individuals wanted to see him. Newspaper reporters wanted a story, and lawyers interested in the case were anxious to see him. And there were plenty of people who just wanted to catch a glimpse of the charismatic Chester Gillette.

For Sheriff John Richards, the situation was intolerable. This endless parade of visitors was interfering with the daily operation of his jail. Something had to be done and done quickly. It was decided to kick Chester upstairs and out of the way. His new cell would be on the second floor in the far right corner. Here, Chester would have a double cell all to himself. In true Chester Gillette fashion, he slept in one cell and, ever the dandy, used the other as his walk-in closet. For a homier touch, he decorated the cell walls with pictures of outdoor scenes torn from the pages of magazines

Above: The Gillette cell in the 1834 Herkimer County Jail today, a highlight of tours of the building. *Editors' collection.*

Right: A photograph of Chester Gillette taken by Herkimer photographer Albert Zintsmaster after Gillette's arrest. *Courtesy of Herkimer County Historical Society.*

and—no surprise here—pictures of girls. Chester would remain in this cell for the remainder of the summer and throughout his trial, which lasted from November 11 to December 4, 1906. Convicted of first-degree murder, he was sentenced to die in the electric chair at Auburn Prison.

When Chester Gillette boarded the train in Herkimer on December 12, 1906, he left behind an odd legacy. Although he was housed in the Herkimer County Jail for only five months, his cell would be forever referred to as the "Gillette cell."

One of the first to occupy the cell after Chester was one-eyed Alphonso Orlando. On Christmas Eve in 1910, he and three other Italians raided a shanty at the West Shore Limited train station in Mohawk. In the melee that followed, knives were drawn and shots were fired. Orlando managed to get away with a bullet wound to the eye; others staggered away with deep cuts and slashes. Dominic Sangunette, however, was taken to Herkimer Memorial Hospital and died later that night from a gunshot wound. After interviewing several of the participants in this affair, the police determined that Orlando had been the trigger man. He was arrested in Utica and brought to the Herkimer County Jail, where he was immediately brought upstairs to the Gillette cell. Charged with first-degree murder, Orlando, on the advice of his attorney, pled guilty to second-degree murder and was sentenced to twenty years at Auburn, thus escaping the electric chair. His attorney was none other than A.M. Mills, the same attorney who couldn't save Chester Gillette from "Old Sparky."[30]

Perhaps the highest-profile prisoner to occupy the Gillette cell since Chester was Jean Gianini of Poland, New York. When brought to the Gillette cell in March 1914, the sixteen-year-old expressed no remorse as he calmly told authorities how he stuck his schoolteacher, twenty-two-year-old Lida Beecher, with a monkey wrench in the back of the skull and for good measure stabbed the poor woman multiple times. Seemingly unworried about his fate, young Gianini expressed his fascination with being housed in the cell once occupied by Chester Gillette. Confiding to one of the deputies that he expected to "get what Chester Gillette got," Gianini brazenly quipped, "I ain't afraid of the chair."[31] A vigorous defense returned a verdict of not guilty by reason of "criminal imbecility."[32] When brought back to his cell after hearing the verdict, an excited Gianini greeted Sheriff William Stitts.

"Hello, Stitty, well I guess I was a pretty lucky kid, wasn't I?"
"You bet you are," replied Sheriff Stitts.[33]

Jean Gianini. *Editors' collection.*

The sheriff was correct. Jean Gianini was lucky. The presiding judge in the case was Irving R. Devendorf, the same judge who had sent Chester Gillette to the electric chair in Auburn. Had the jury found Gianini guilty, Judge Devendorf most certainly would have sent him to the chair. Gianini was taken from the Gillette cell and sent to the Matteawan Asylum for the Criminally Insane.[34]

In addition to being the oldest resident to occupy the Gillette cell, at age sixty-seven, John Henry House of Columbia Center was perhaps the most ruthless. The multiple-married House (first marriage, divorce; second, death in childbirth; third, suicide under questionable circumstances; and fourth, another divorce) was arrested for the murder of Harriet Schmoll House, wife number five, on June 27, 1924.[35]

Vainly attempting to flee a horrible relationship, Harriet left her husband and sought refuge at the nearby farm of Jacob Shaul. Here she cooked and kept house for Shaul in return for her room and board. The only problem was that the Shaul farm

John Henry House. *Editors' collection.*

wasn't far enough away from her violent husband. On the afternoon of June 27, House went to the Shaul farmhouse and confronted Harriet. The two argued, House later said, over missing farm tools. The six-foot, 185-pound House was too much for the diminutive Harriet. Removing a straight razor from his pocket, House thrust the blade into her abdomen, piercing the liver. He then slashed her violently in the neck. The five-inch-long wound was so deep that it severed the jugular vein as well as the windpipe. House went home and went to bed as if nothing had happened.[36]

When Jacob Shaul returned home later in the afternoon, a grisly scene awaited him. He immediately contacted the authorities, and they in turn rushed to the scene. House was taken into custody without incident. In fact, he never bothered to clean the blood off his boots or his trousers. Brought to the Gillette cell, John Henry House not only included all the gory details in his confession but also added, "I left her kicking and bleeding on the floor." When deputies asked him if he was sorry for what he had done, House expressed absolutely no remorse. "Sorry I killed her? No Sir! I's do it again if I had the chance."[37] He claimed self-defense, but the butcher knife Harriet supposedly threatened him with was never found.

While angry neighbors in Columbia Center cried out for the electric chair, the district attorney made plans to take the case to the grand jury. Inside the Gillette cell, John Henry House made plans of his own. On the morning of July 10, 1924, deputies bringing breakfast to the second floor of the jail discovered House's lifeless body hanging from the gas jet inside his cell.

"Thank God," exclaimed Mrs. James Schmoll, Harriet's sister-in-law. "That's the best news I have heard in a week."[38] John Henry House may have cheated the electric chair, but the taxpayers of Herkimer were saved the cost of a long trial.

In the 1920s, the Gillette cell housed two stranglers. The case of Thomas Wagner of Little Falls was indeed unfortunate. Separated from his wife, the former Golda Hotaling, for one year, the distraught twenty-two-year-old Wagner desperately wanted to reconcile. On August 31, 1926, Wagner went to her boardinghouse room at 337 South Ann Street and confronted his estranged spouse. In a heated exchange, Golda refused to return home to her husband. When she began to scream, Thomas, in a blind rage, silenced her the only way he knew how. He put his hands around her neck and began to choke her. She collapsed. Fearing the worst, Wagner went immediately to the police. He told them what had transpired and believed that Golda was still alive. The police, and later the coroner, concluded that the nineteen-year-old had been strangled.[39]

Apparently, business was slow that summer at the Herkimer County Jail. When Wagner was brought to the Gillette cell, he discovered that he was the only person housed on the second floor. From all outward appearances, Thomas Wagner adjusted well to his new surroundings. He had few visitors and bided his time by reading newspapers, especially those that had to do with his crime. Found guilty of manslaughter, Wagner was sentenced to "not less than 10 or more than 20 years" at Auburn Prison.[40]

The following year, on June 11, 1927, Herkimer resident Walter Jereux, a local bootlegger, was brought to the same cell, charged with the murder of his wife, Amy. He claimed that he was innocent, that he was downstairs when his wife, who was upstairs, fell on the floor. The fall, he maintained, caused the injuries to her neck that proved to be fatal. It was a good story, but his ten-year-old daughter, Helen, told a better story. When she took the witness stand, she testified that "Papa beat mother over the head with a hammer and then chocked her."[41] Her testimony convinced the jury of her father's guilt. From the Gillette cell, Jereux was whisked away to Auburn Prison, where reservations had been made for his seven-and-a-half-year stay.

The following decade, the 1930s, proved to be a busy time for the Herkimer County Jail. It almost appeared as if a revolving, steel-barred door had been installed in the Gillette cell. As one person was convicted and sent to prison, another arrived to take his place.

Sixty-year-old Michael Camerano may not have been one of the most infamous men to await trial in the Gillette cell, but he was one of the most expensive. Accused of the shotgun murder of Leroy Sweet on October 26, 1926, in Frankfort, Camerano made his way to Long Island, then to Boston and finally back to his hometown in Padula, Italy. It took four years for the authorities to locate him and file extradition papers. This was no small feat when one considers the political climate in Italy. Camerano was the only Italian citizen extradited to the United States by the Mussolini regime.[42]

Toward the end of March 1931, the family of Leroy Sweet got justice. Encouraged by his attorney to plead guilty to second-degree murder, Michael Camerano was saved from the electric chair and was sentenced to Auburn for twenty years. Meanwhile, the taxpayers of Herkimer County were saddled with a lot of bills.

First, there was the cost of the round-trip voyage to Italy for Sheriff J. Collingswood Rasbach and Deputy Adam Allen. They probably didn't travel first class, but the bill still had to be paid. As for Camerano, the cost for bringing him back to America to stand trial was less expensive. It was a one-way ticket, but he did get room service while he was confined to the ship's brig for the duration of the voyage. The Bronx detective who located Camerano in Italy and later notified officials in Herkimer County presented the board of supervisors with a bill of $5,860 for services rendered. The board scaled it back to $4,150. After that, it seemed like everyone associated with the case wanted a piece of the action. John Nellis of Cold Brook wanted $60 for night-guard duty at the cell, and a translator demanded $105 to transcribe the legal papers that accompanied Camerano. Even the barber wanted his fair share. Ed Grenier of the City Barber Shop claimed that six shaves for $6 was worth his time, and he wanted to get paid just like everybody else. Encouraged by his attorney to plead guilty to second-degree murder, Camerano not only avoided the electric chair but also saved the taxpayers of Herkimer County a costly trial. Camerano was sentenced to twenty years at Auburn.[43]

Camerano was no sooner on the train to Auburn than the Gillette cell got a little crowded. In 1905, thirty-year-old Anthony "Tony" Bilger of Salisbury found himself behind bars in the county lockup for a minor offense. When he returned to the jail in 1932, the charge was much more serious. On February 17, Bilger, in a highly intoxicated state, had a fatal altercation with a neighbor, William Knox. As the story goes, the two were engaged in a wrestling match in which Knox got the better of his drunken opponent. As Knox walked away, Bilger grabbed a shotgun and fired twice. While some newspapers reported that Knox had his head almost blown off, others claimed that the shot tore apart the victim's chest. At any rate, the

Sheriff Leo Lawrence with Mike Camerano outside the Herkimer County Jail. *Courtesy of Herkimer County Historical Society.*

From left to right: Anthony Bilger, Sheriff Leo Lawrence, Anthony DiPiazza and turnkey Charles Daniel in the Gillette cell. *Courtesy of Herkimer County Historical Society.*

only thing that really mattered was that Knox was dead and sixty-five-year-old Anthony Bilger had been arrested.[44]

When Tony Bilger was brought to the Gillette cell, he was introduced to another Tony. On November 20, 1931, Anthony "Tony" DiPiazza was arrested in Frankfort for the murder of Nicholas "Coco" DiMaggio on Columbus Day. Late in the evening of October 12, 1931, DiMaggio was walking home on Railroad Street having just left a card game at Benny Zito's. Walking beside him was Tony DiPiazza. Taking a step or two back, DiPiazza took a gun from his coat pocket and fired five slugs into the head of DiMaggio. The authorities considered several of the card players that night as "persons of interest." When one alibi after another was verified, it looked as if DiPiazza was their man. After sixty-seven days in jail, DiPiazza signed a full confession.[45]

Apparently, the latest occupants of the Gillette cell got along well. Bilger enjoyed being serenaded with the Italian ballads sung by DiMaggio. In return, the native of Frankfort seemed to be captivated by the stories Bilger told about the country life of Salisbury. The two Tonys were indicted for murder on the same day, March 17, 1932, and each awaited their turn before the judge and jury.[46]

On April 4, 1932, Tony Bilger, on the advice of his attorney, pled guilty to second-degree murder and was sentenced to between six and twelve years at Auburn Prison. His cellmate went to trial toward the end of the month.[47] On May 7, 1932, Anthony DiPiazza was found guilty of second-degree murder and sentenced to from twenty years to life at Auburn.

When twenty-year-old Hildreth Burroughs of Little Falls was brought to the Gillette cell, he behaved in much the same way as had another Little Falls native, Thomas Wagner. Burroughs kept to himself and spent most of his time reading. What he was reading was anyone's guess; you would like to think he was reading the Bible.

In the early hours of April 6, 1935, Little Falls police were summoned to the Gilbert Knitting Mill. The body of sixty-eight-year-old John Ober, the night watchman, was lying in a pool of blood. A heavy wood bobbin had been used to crush Ober's skull. The police had a suspect in mind, but it took about three months of investigating to make the arrest. When twenty-year-old Hildreth Burroughs was arrested and taken to the Herkimer County Jail, the public recoiled in horror. "The lure of easy money and an aversion to work causes the snuffing out of a useful life," was how one editorial responded. Burroughs had robbed Ober of thirty-three dollars and a pocket watch. "Bad companions and a warped slant on the objects of life seem to have led him to the unenviable place he now occupies"—the Gillette cell.[48]

Two weeks into his trial for first-degree murder, Burroughs did an about-face and pled guilty. He was sentenced to a minimum of ten years and not more than twenty in Attica Prison.

Often, when those who have served their sentence—as people like to say, "paid their debt to society"—are released from prison, they choose not to return home. Some relocate to other villages or counties, while others move out of state. When Anthony DiPiazza was released from Auburn after serving eighteen years for the murder of Nicholas DiMaggio, he relocated to the Little Italy section of St. Louis, Missouri. The quiet life he led in his new surroundings, however, was suddenly interrupted in late July 1964. His twenty-year-old grandson, Bennie, paid him a visit. Benedict "Bennie" DiPiazza had been in and out of trouble for several years for stalking Noreen Jones of Ilion. After two weeks in St. Louis, Bennie returned to Frankfort and continued to stalk Noreen.[49] On August 27, 1964, he chased Noreen into the Frankfort police station and shot her six times. He was arrested, sent to the Herkimer County Jail and placed in the same cell his grandfather had once occupied.

This is by no means a complete list of those individuals who at one time or another awaited their day in court while sitting in the Chester Gillette cell. Anyone could be and certainly was detained in this particular section of the second floor of the jail. When the jail experienced any overcrowding, the cell was used. Often, when prisoners were received from other counties, they were tucked away in this corner cell. At times, a prisoner was housed in this cell if he was troublesome or incorrigible. No matter who occupied the Gillette cell, one fact remains: only one prisoner paid with his life, and that was Chester.

22
CRIMINAL MELODRAMA

by Barbara Dunadee

Raymond Mulford spent almost all of the last year of his life in the Sing Sing Death House, incarcerated there since January 22, 1921, for the murder of Abraham Yellen in Buffalo. His plea to New York's governor, Nathan L. Miller, to commute his sentence had been rejected and with it his last flicker of hope. Death by electrocution would come on January 12, 1922, for the five-foot, eight-inch, blue-eyed, brown-haired man, just two weeks shy of his twenty-eighth birthday. On the prison's receiving blotter, Mulford listed his address as 312½ North Washington Street in Herkimer, but the truth was that he hadn't lived there for a while. Ironically, his last glimpses of his hometown were through the windows of the New York Central train transporting him and another convicted murderer on the 350-mile journey from Buffalo across New York State to Ossining, where Sing Sing is located. A newspaperman accompanying the group as the train clamored along the tracks that dissected the village witnessed Mulford pointing to the Snell Lumber Yard, admitting to those nearby that it was there that he had committed his first crime.

What paths taken by Mulford led him to be in Buffalo in November 1920, when this heinous act was perpetrated? The answer to this question involves piecing together a lifetime of illicit behavior that spiraled out of control. We are given a peek into the shadows of Mulford's hidden existence through the testimony of the prosecution's star witness during his 1921 murder trial: Lillian Gusse, who had been his girlfriend. She detailed a year-

Mulford mugshots. *New York State Archives; Albany, New York; Elmira Reformatory Biographical Registers and Receiving Plotters. Series Number B0141.*

long crime spree by Mulford and his gang involving numerous holdups and armed robberies in a long list of cities including Detroit, Cleveland, Akron, Toledo, St. Louis and Lancaster. They targeted lucrative jewelry stores and businesses. The gang had evaded capture, leaving the authorities scratching their heads as to who they were. However, in Buffalo, their luck ran out. Here, the real truth about Raymond Mulford was brought to light. What was revealed was a portrait of a man who was unprincipled and dangerous.

Raymond Francois Mulford was born in Bainbridge, New York, on January 27, 1894, to Clarence and Ellen Mulford. When he was a young boy, his parents split up, with Ellen remarrying Everett Mitchell and moving her family to Mitchell's home in Herkimer. Ellen and Everett would welcome two daughters, half-sisters to Raymond and his older brother, Claude.

Raymond's first arrest came in 1906 at the age of twelve when he, big brother Claude and several other boys were charged in connection with a series of break-ins in the Newport area. The police found a large stash of stolen goods in their possession. The Mulford boys were sent to the Industrial School at Rochester, where they spent four years before returning home. Raymond Mulford was sixteen.

He left Herkimer in his late teens, becoming a drifter who never established roots in one place or held a job for very long. He worked as a trolley motorman in Rutledge, Vermont, in 1913. Here, he smooth-talked his way into convincing Clara May Lashier that he was the love of her life. He married her, only to leave her within months. In 1914, he was sought by the Gloversville Police in connection with a robbery of fifty dollars from a local restaurant where he had been a night chef. A warrant was issued for his arrest, but he was never apprehended. On November 3 of that year, he married Irene George in Oneida. This marriage eventually turned sour. Rumors of Mulford's mistreatment of Irene would surface during his 1921 murder trial.

In January 1915, Mulford was sent to the Elmira Reformatory for second-degree grand larceny and carrying an unregistered gun after he stole items belonging to coworkers at a farm in Marcy. He was released in April on parole and given ten days to find employment. Instead, he skipped town. Another warrant was then issued, this time for parole violation.

Mulford was in Palmer, Massachusetts, during the early-morning hours of June 13, 1916, when he and another man were surprised by a policeman while trying to jimmy a lock to a store. Mulford exchanged gunshots with him, and in the melee, the officer was wounded. Mulford escaped capture, but his accomplice was caught. This time, the warrant for his arrest cited attempted breaking and entering as well as assault with the intent to kill.

On November 29, 1916, another woman fell victim to his deceptive charm. Helen Roder married Mulford, who called himself Roy Jones, in Hartford, Connecticut, where he ran a boardinghouse. Just took two months later, Mulford/Jones left town with several hundred dollars of his wife's money. Helen placed ads in local newspapers searching for her missing husband for four years, hoping to get some support for herself and their daughter. Her search ended when she received news about her estranged husband's arrest on murder charges.

According to his World War I draft registration card, Mulford was residing in Kansas City, Missouri, in June 1917. By 1918, he was in Detroit working in a restaurant and courting Mary Delavon, whom he married on April 25. The ink was barely dry on this fourth marriage certificate before the three-time bigamist left the state.

While in Buffalo in 1919, he made the acquaintance of twenty-two-year-old waitress Lillian Gusse, who had recently left her husband. For almost a year, the couple lived together as man and wife while subsisting on what they could steal. They moved frequently to new locations to avoid the police, often hopping on boxcars to get from one town to the next. Gusse, sometimes armed with Mulford's gun, served as a lookout for his thefts. She continued in this post even after Mulford added two young recruits, Floyd C. Slover, twenty-two, and Harold Webber, twenty-three, to assist in his criminal activity. Almost all of the puzzle pieces to Mulford's self-destruction had now fallen into place as Mulford and Gusse arrived back in Buffalo in November 1920 accompanied by Slover and Webber.

The gang took up residence at a North Division Street boardinghouse with little spare cash in anyone's pockets. It was Thanksgiving Day, November 25, 1920. Gusse and Mulford had had a heated argument the night before concerning their lack of money for a Thanksgiving meal. In the morning, when things had cooled down a bit, Mulford said that he would have a decent meal for her and left with his men to carry through with plans for a new heist. Gusse did not accompany them.

Mulford once again put his outlaw instincts to use as he and his two cohorts prowled for easy money, looking for vulnerable prey and an advantageous moment to pounce. The day would prove to be a fateful one for the gang as well as for forty-seven-year-old second-hand clothing store owner Abraham Yellen. Mr. Yellen's haberdashery business had existed in a busy commercial area at 194 Seneca Street for over twenty years. A well-respected member of the community, Yellen had emigrated from Poland in 1896 with his wife and three boys.

At 9:30 a.m., Mulford and Slover entered Yellen's store. Webber remained outside to serve as lookout. Slover asked to try on a coat. The merchant obliged by helping him into one. Slover and Mulford started to walk out the door with Slover still wearing the coat. Yellen blocked their exit, refusing to let them leave with the merchandise. He grabbed for the coat as a scuffle erupted. Slover pulled out a .32-caliber revolver that Mulford had given him earlier and fired three shots at Yellen, hitting him in the hand, chest and abdomen. The thieves raced out of the store with Yellen staggering after them. Adjacent shopkeepers and customers turned to see Yellen collapsing to the ground while three men took off down the street.

Officer Daniel M. Condren of the Buffalo Police Department was around the corner from Yellen's store when he heard the repeated loud pop of multiple gunshots. He hurried in the direction of the sounds. Once he was on the scene, eyewitnesses pointed to the escaping bandits, and he took off after them. While lagging a distance behind, he saw the three men climb a fence and disappear. Not about to give up on his quarry, he jumped onto the running board of a passing automobile. Its speed helped him get to a location to overtake the suspects. After disembarking, he spotted them standing in front of a nearby store. The crooks were not looking in his direction as he positioned himself to get the drop on them while silently taking out his service revolver to zero in on his target. Officer Condren surprised them and single-handedly captured the three men before they could turn on him. Soon, police vehicles arrived with sirens blaring to assist with the arrests.

The next stop was the Erie County Jail, where the suspects were questioned. Detectives found the men uncooperative, giving the bogus names they had been using. Sorting truth from lies took a considerable amount of time. Officers were sent to the boardinghouse at 236 North Division Street, where Lillian Gusse was taken into custody. Disturbing news arrived at the jail in the afternoon. The store owner, Abraham Yellen, had succumbed to his wounds, dying at 2:45 p.m. at Columbus Hospital. The trio now faced murder charges that, with a guilty verdict, carried the death penalty.

At first reluctant to discuss her connection to the accused murderers, Lillian Gusse soon opened up about what had transpired between herself and the gang members in the hours, weeks and months before the murder, including detailed accounts of their activities. She continued to spew incriminating information to the district attorney. Her revelations were especially damaging to the gang's ringleader, Raymond Mulford, who had given the orders that others followed. She also exposed secrets from her paramour's turbulent past to which she was privy, stretching back to his early twenties. The next day, a judge ordered that Gusse be held as a material witness with bail set at $2,500. Her story made headline news in Buffalo and beyond. Dozens of newspapers sent reporters to get the scoop by covering every angle of the unfolding events surrounding the murder.

A court arraignment for Mulford, Slover and Webber was attempted on Saturday, November 27. In the courtroom already seated were two of Yellen's sons, J. Zelig "Jack" Yellen and Max M. Yellen. The defendants entered the courtroom with Mulford and Webber handcuffed together and Slover handcuffed to a detective. Simultaneously, the angry Yellen brothers left their seats to rush at Floyd Stover, tackling him, punching him in the face and breaking his nose. The brothers were pulled away from the suspect and then were immediately arrested for contempt of court and led away. As a result of the disturbance, the judicial proceedings were postponed until December 7. The charges against the Yellen brothers would later be dropped.

The sketches of the major players in the murder trial. *Buffalo Commercial*, "Mulford's Fate Went to the Jury This Afternoon," January 5, 1921.

Extra police protection was given to the prisoners so that their next court appearances were carried out without incident. A grand jury indicted all three for first-degree murder on December 13. Separate trials for the accused would be held, with Mulford going before a jury first, then Slover and, finally, Webber.

Mulford's trial began on January 5, 1921. The courtroom and hallways of the city hall were packed with throngs of newsmen and curious onlookers. Supreme Court justice Louis W. Marcus presided over the trial. District Attorney Guy B. Moore presented the state's case. Representing Mulford was attorney Bart J. Shanahan. Several eyewitnesses were called by the district attorney to describe what they had seen. A truck driver passing the store at the time of the shooting observed Mulford running with two other men out of the store. A nearby merchant identified Slover as the shooter and Mulford and Webber as accomplices.

Lillian Gusse, wearing a black silk dress, suede shoes and a large black picture hat, took the stand to answer DA Moore's questions, repeating much of what she had told beforehand to the authorities. She described scores of store robberies and holdups masterminded by Mulford in cities throughout the states bordering the Great Lakes. Mulford would supply the gang members with guns to be used to intimidate victims or to protect themselves against capture. While admitting to being present when these felonies occurred, she emphatically denied taking an active part in them, except to warn the gang if someone was approaching. A repentant Gusse confessed to shooting a man in Gardenville who had tried to apprehend her during a failed robbery attempt. She fired several shots at her pursuer in the dark and, hearing a loud groan, knew she had hit him.

The skilled prosecutor prodded his witness to elaborate on what had occurred in the apartment on the morning of the murder. She said Mulford was getting ready for his next job, as he felt Thanksgiving would be an opportune day. They desperately needed cash, and Mulford had promised her a nice holiday meal. When he left, she thought the gang would be heading to the jewelry store they had previously checked out.

When it came time for the defense, attorney Shanahan called both Slover and Webber as witnesses, hoping that one of them would portray Mulford as an innocent bystander. However, neither man answered questions, instead remaining silent to avoid self-incrimination. Mulford, battling to save his life, testified in his own defense. He told about his two youthful arrests, explaining that he was no angel but was not a murderer. He bore no blame for Yellen's death, as he had followed Slover into the store out of curiosity, not knowing that Slover was going to shoot the merchant.

In its cross-examination, the prosecution came down hard with a barrage of questions for Mulford. The cool, confident defendant became defiant, sneering at the prosecutor, who repeatedly asked about what had gone on inside Yellen's store. He picked apart Mulford's answers, riling him enough that he contradicted some of his earlier responses. The questions included, Why he had gone into the store? If he had very little money, how could he expect to buy a coat? Why did Slover have his gun? Why didn't Mulford try to stop Slover from shooting Yellen? Mulford hurled back answers, trying to stick to his story. Moore then expanded his line of questioning to include Mulford's past indiscretions. By using information gained from Gusse's testimony as well as newly received in-state and out-of-state warrants naming the defendant, Moore had plenty to confront the witness about. Mulford was asked if he shot a policeman, took money from an employer or orchestrated robberies in numerous cities and towns. An angry defendant refused to answer questions that were not about the present case. Moore continued, inquiring about Mulford's past relationships Had he tried to poison his pregnant wife seven years before in Oneida? Was he married to the woman in Hartford, Connecticut, who claimed to be his wife? Mulford again refused to answer. This aggressive questioning continued for the rest of the day and part of the next day.

Once Mulford's grilling was concluded, attorney Shanahan had Mulford explain to the jury that he had not poisoned his wife and that he knew Helen Roder from Hartford but was not married to her. Both lawyers then made their closing arguments. Justice Marcus addressed the jury, informing them about the differences between first- and second-degree murder and manslaughter. He also pointed out that a murder occurring during the act of committing a felony constituted murder in the first degree and that accomplices were equally as guilty as the individual who fired the gun. The jury was then allowed to begin its deliberations.

Fifty minutes later, the court was reconvened as a decision had been made. Raymond Francois Mulford was found guilty of first-degree murder in the killing of Abraham Yellen. Sentencing was delayed until after the remaining two defendants had had their trials.

A dejected Mulford returned to his cell to anxiously await his fate. During that two-week interval, he was counseled by a minister, who contacted his mother in Herkimer, hoping that she could visit him and bring him some solace. Ellen Mitchell wrote that she believed her son was innocent but that her poor health prevented her from making the journey. Mulford tried to communicate with his long-forgotten wife in Oneida, but no response came.

Another note was sent to Helen Roder, who did reply. She had decided to honor his request and bring her little girl to meet him.

Slover became the second of the accused to be convicted of first-degree murder, on January 14, eight days after Mulford's conviction on January 6. Harold Webber's case was never brought before a jury, as he accepted the prosecutor's deal to plead guilty to second-degree murder and accept a twenty-year-to-life prison term.

The largest crowd to ever pack into city hall gathered on January 21, 1921, for the sentencing. Harold Webber went before Justice Marcus first and was ordered to be sent to Auburn Prison to begin his agreed-to punishment. Raymond Mulford and Floyd Slover each were sentenced to death by electrocution, set for March 7, 1921, at Sing Sing Prison.

The next day, all three prisoners boarded an eastbound train. Webber was escorted off at Auburn, some 130 miles from Buffalo. The remaining prisoners' ride to their final destination would take much of the day. Several newspaper reporters accompanied the Sing Sing group on their last ride. Arriving at the prison, Mulford and Slover were taken to the Death House, a separate part of the Sing Sing complex reserved for those slated for execution.

March 7 came and went as Mulford appealed his conviction. Helen Roder carried through with her promise and brought her four-year-old daughter to see her father. Mulford's prospects for staying alive grew dimmer as the year progressed. After his request for a new trial was rejected, an execution date was set for the second week in January 1922. Letters from his half-sisters lifted his spirits. They wrote to encourage their brother to remain strong. The prison chaplain met with Mulford to help him cope with his impending death.

On January 11, his hair was shaved. He was given a special shirt to wear with slits in the sides for straps to be inserted. On January 12, the governor refused to step in and block the execution. That evening, at approximately 11:00 p.m., Warden Lewis E. Lawes guided the condemned man down the hall, opening "the little green door" into a specially equipped area designated for electrocutions. Raymond J. McCarthy, a reporter for the *Buffalo Enquirer*, was in an adjacent viewing room separated by glass and bore witness to the convict's last minutes. The chaplain prayed with Mulford. The prisoner was stoic as the attendants fastened the bands around him connecting him to the electric chair. "Good bye boys, Pray for me," were his last words. Lawes gave the signal for the switch to be flipped, sending a surge of high-voltage current throughout Mulford's body for a duration of two minutes. After his vitals were checked, it was determined that his heart had stopped beating.

Mulford was declared dead at 11:15 p.m. Later, since no one claimed his body, he was buried on prison grounds.

Frank Slover shared a similar fate, with his electrocution taking place on February 2, three weeks after Mulford's. Others whose lives were intertwined with Mulford's fared differently. Harold Webber was released in 1931 after serving twenty years at the Auburn Prison. He was forty-three. Lillian Gusse was set free from Erie County Jail in March 1921, less than two months after Mulford's conviction, clutching the hand of her husband, with whom she had reconciled. Her sentence for assault in Gardensville was reduced to time served, with DA Moore taking note of the assistance she had given in the Yellen murder trial. Officer Condren was promoted to detective within weeks of his daring capture. He died twenty-three years later of natural causes, forever remembered as a hero. Jack Yellen, the son of the murder victim arrested for attacking Slover in court, was a budding lyricist and songwriter. He would go on to fame and fortune with such songs as "Happy Days Are Here Again" and "Ain't She Sweet."

Raymond Mulford was quoted in an interview as blaming the women in his life for what went wrong. A chorus of voices from his past, those who had to pick up the pieces of their lives after he was gone, would find exception to his statement. The term *sociopath* comes to mind when trying to explain his behavior. He lacked a moral compass, disregarding laws and exploiting other people to obtain what he wanted. He was a master manipulator, reinventing who he was to suit the needs of the situation, as well as aligning himself with people he could control. He was a Lothario, attractive to the opposite sex. But hiding under his pleasing exterior was a scoundrel who abused women. The early 1920s lacked a communication network for law-enforcement agencies to quickly exchange bulletins about desperate fugitives. Mulford was able to use this to his advantage to continue the modus operandi of leaving one town when the cops were closing in or when things weren't going according to his liking and moving to another place, shedding yesterday's problems to restart his shady way of living. All of this went into what was the truly unprincipled and dangerous Raymond F. Mulford.

23

SHOOTOUT AT CAMP UTICA IN OLD FORGE

BY SUSAN PERKINS

On January 31, 1927, at a speakeasy located at 214 West 103rd Street in New York City, a holdup by four gunmen was taking place when Patrolman James Masterson, who was in plain clothes and had been in the building, responded to the scene. Walter "Tip" Murray (aka Walter Tipping) shot Masterson twice while the gunmen continued to rob the patrons, taking $1,800 in money and jewelry.

Peter Seiler was a member of the gang and, according to a newspaper report, stopped by Masterson, who was lying unconscious, and said, "Give it to the big bum, boys." Tipping sent a third bullet into the patrolman's body, and the four thugs hurried away. Masterson died less than twenty-four hours later.

Seiler was friends with Grace Peterson of Forest Hills, Long Island, who, with her husband, George, owned a camp in Old Forge called Camp Utica. After the robbery, Grace made a call to someone in Old Forge to ask them to turn the water on at the camp. Peter Seiler and Walter Tipping, along with Grace Peterson, went to Camp Utica to hide out at the isolated cabin, which was located on South Shore Road between Old Forge and Inlet. Their location was soon revealed to authorities by a woman who was referred to as "Sarah." The reason for her action? Jealousy of Grace Peterson.

New York City detectives, led by Thomas Martin and including Thomas Brady, Steven Donahue and Francis Tied, along with New York State Troopers George Cowburn and Corporal Whitwer, were on the move to the

Above: Camp Utica scene after the shootout. *Courtesy of Herkimer County Historical Society*.

Left: Peter Seiler handcuffed. *Courtesy of Herkimer County Historical Society*.

town of Webb. It was February 8, 1927, when they closed in on the camp in the early-morning light. The officers had planned to take the gunmen in their sleep. However, they didn't plan on "Lady," Grace Peterson's Airedale dog, who sensed their presence and started barking, alerting the residents in the camp. With the camp surrounded, Martin and Brady broke down the door, calling out to Seiler and Tipping to surrender. Tipping immediately opened fire, wounding Martin in the right wrist. He retreated to the side of the camp and began shooting through the window at Tipping. One of the shots struck Tipping in the temple, killing him instantly. Peter Seiler was captured in another room of the camp when Detective Brady tackled him and knocked a revolver from his hand. Grace Peterson, who was found in the room with Seiler, was arrested for harboring fugitives.

Grace, held on $50,000 bail, was not cooperating with the police. They tried to get her to tell them where the other two men involved in the robbery were at the speakeasy, but she remained uncooperative. The police were also trying to figure out the mystery of the house where Grace lived in Forest Hills. It was learned that three women had lived there for some time and that they made and received mysterious telephone calls. Some of the calls were traced, which led to the camp. Young male callers frequented the home where the four women lived. One of the women, Rebecca Griffin, was arrested at the home and questioned. It was learned that Grace's husband, George Peterson, was often out of town. He was a horse trainer at Hialeah Track in Miami, Florida, where he was at the time of the incident. Grace said her husband knew she was going to the camp, but he thought it was for her health.

As for Peter Seiler, he confessed to three other restaurant holdups with Tipping. He may have been implicated in eleven others. Seiler was sentenced to die in the electric chair on December 16, 1927, for his role in the killing of Patrolman Masterson. His final written statement read as follows:

> *Gentlemen, you are about to see an innocent man die. I did not kill anybody. I have proved beyond doubt, and the Appeal Court will concur with me, that I did not shoot anyone. Still, the State will take my life. Is this justice? The Appeal Court recommends a change in the law that I was convicted under. That doesn't do me any good, but I will gladly die if my death will bring about the change that the Appeal Court recommends by legislation. I will die with a smile; my conscience is clear and I bear no ill will or malice. This is but a gateway to eternity. All I wish is a kind thought or prayer for my dear mother, father and sister. They are the real*

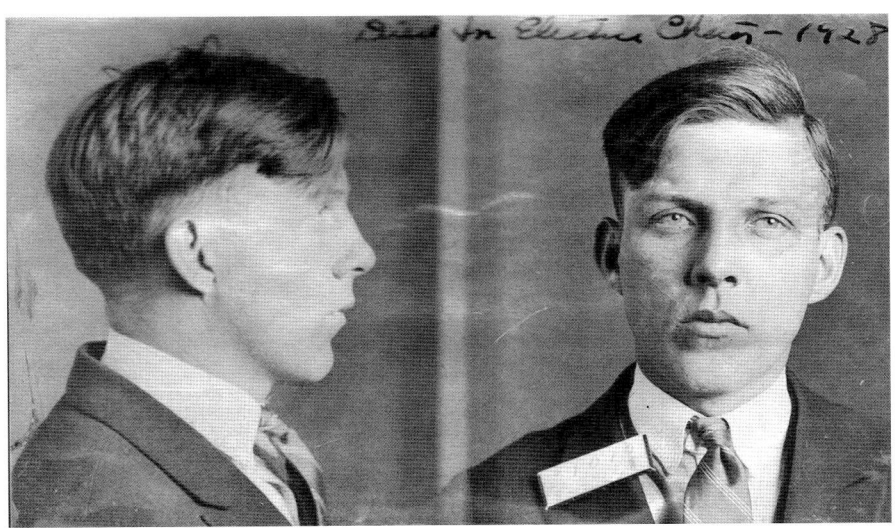

Peter Seiler mugshot. *Courtesy of Herkimer County Historical Society.*

martyrs. God bless then and have mercy on their soul. I will go now where I will find justice, tempered with mercy, from which there is no appeal. God bless you all. Thank you.

Seiler was strapped in the chair immediately after the reading and was electrocuted. Warden Lewis E. Lawes, newspapermen and Drs. C.C. Sweet and James Kearny, official surgeons, witnessed the execution.

24

RECOLLECTIONS OF A WICKED BOY IN HERKIMER

by Det Smada (taken from an interview in July 2020)

Growing up in Herkimer in the 1940s was a very interesting time for me. There were lots of adventures, which I'll try to relate.

Being caught climbing up the fire escape of the Masonic Temple on Main Street. It may have been my idea just to see what was going on inside. There were four of us. I'm not sure how our parish pastor, Father McCarthy, found out, but he called us in and read the riot act about being on Masonic property and that we were all probably going to hell. My friend lived across the street, and we used to play around that area. We just wanted to go in and see what was going on, because it was such a secret place—for young kids, too much to resist. What's going on there? We saw nothing. There was no way to look in. We were dismayed, because we found we couldn't see anything going on. Curtains were closed in the window. Someone yelled at us, and we got down and ran away.

If it wasn't bad enough that we got in trouble at the Masonic Temple, we used to walk and play by the Herkimer County Jail's screened windows—often, we would rattle the windows, laugh and yell. One day, the sheriff, Charlie Malsan (1903–1970), came out and grabbed us on the back of the shirts and put us in a cell. At this point, I may have been crying. Of course, he left us only for fifteen minutes, gave us a big lecture and said, "This time I'm not telling your parents, but if you do it again, I am going to call them." We never did it again.

Herkimer Masonic Temple on North Main Street. *Editors' collection.*

On a brighter note, one of the exciting things three of my friends and I did was, when the war ended, my friend's father took us over to the Herkimer County Courthouse, and we ran up to the bell tower and we were able to ring the bell at the end of World War II. I don't mind giving the names of the kids in this case—Jack Manion, Tommy Fagan and Francis Reardon.

I can remember as a kid hanging out a lot down at the Herkimer County Airport [located where the New York State Department of Transportation now is on Fifth Avenue], always hoping that someday someone would give me a ride. I came up one day, and one of the pilot owners came over and said, "Hey kid, you ever been up in an airplane?" I said, "No," and he said, "Come on, I'm taking a short drive." When I was getting in the plane, he said, "You look scared—don't worry kid, I've never left anyone up there yet." Which at the time made sense to me. This was the first of many rides. I got to know one of the plane owners, and he took an interest in me and I started going with him on plane trips. I joined the Civil Air Patrol and actually learned to fly an airplane at fifteen years old. I can remember great fear when I was able to take off from the Herkimer Airport myself—stayed up for a half an hour and land without incident. I did very well. The landing field was between the canal and railroad tracks with power lines—when you'd come up, you would come down the canal, and when you reached the South Washington Street corner with a big water tower, you would zero in on the water tower and the railroad—follow the railroad until you were over the power lines, drop your speed and land and hope you didn't go into the canal.

At one time, we were having a family get-together in Syracuse, and there was not enough room for all of us, so I told my sister to come down to the airport, and Mr. Deck will fly us to Syracuse. My sister got in the back seat of the plane, and I got in the front. She said, "Where's Mr. Deck?" I started the engine, and off we flew. She almost died. I said, "Don't you dare tell Mother," because they picked us up at the airport. I was fifteen.

Speaking of the canal, on the Mohawk River side of the canal there was a water gate lock, and as a young kid, you were nobody if you didn't climb across the top of that lock. You had to jump over to get on the cement abutment, go up the stairs and then climb up the side of the lock and over the top of it and on the other side. You had to come back the same way. I did it—it was scary. I was about thirteen years old. The other coming-of-age test was the South Washington Street Bridge. I can recall the times when you were nobody if you didn't jump off that bridge into the Mohawk River. I did that once. That was enough for me.

I was the perfect student, but some of my friends were certainly not. We had this plan—one of our friend's father owned a farm, and he was old enough to drive a truck, and he brought the truck down with hay in the back, parked it up against the building. We were in class, and that was my job, to tell the teacher it was warm, "can I open the window?," which I did, and back to my seat. One of the students said, "I can't stand it any longer," jumped out the window and into the truck. The teacher almost died. There was a lot of confusion. The student who jumped came back in, went to the boys' room and came out and asked, "What is going on?" "I thought you jumped out the window," said the teacher, Maude Rolls (we called her Tootsie, not to her face, of course)—and all the other teachers and principal looked at her like she was crazy. I thought that was a terrible thing. (Ha Ha.)

I'm told during one Halloween, a group of bad actors went to Brookwood Park, carried the portable restroom down and put it in the middle of German Street. It was probably Monk Manion's gang. He lived on North Caroline

South Washington Street Bridge over the Barge Canal. *Courtesy of Herkimer County Historical Society.*

Street. He had a bunch of guys who were a little bit older than we were. They played a lot of sports. They scared us, because they were bigger, much like Scott Farkus in the *Christmas Story* movie.

I can remember one of the daring things we did. There was a coal house on Albany Street, and they had slides from the second floor to the bottom floor inside the storage bins. I can remember we would sneak in there, climb up to the second floor and slide down the coal bins. I got caught. One time, sliding down, there was a nail, and I hit it and ripped the rear end of my pants, and I had to go home and tell my mother what happened.

We also used to hang around the Ford garage a lot [where Tractor Supply is now]. My neighbor was a mechanic there. I was only about fourteen years old, but the manager thought I was older. I learned to drive quite young. Oftentimes, he might say, "Here, Ted, here's a license plate, put it on this car. I'll follow you over someplace to deliver it." It was fortunate I never got pulled over without a license. It didn't seem to worry me at the time. To attest to my driving ability, I wanted to get my license, so I signed up for driver training. When we got the car out, it was my turn to drive. I drove four or five blocks, and the teacher, Doug Anderson, said, "Pull over by the school and get out the car and go back to school because you can drive as good as I can."

I grew up in a large family, five boys and three girls. My older brother Don always told my mother he spent many nights at the library. Across from the library was the town pool hall, known as "The Gut." We found out that my brother Don was actually spending most of those nights in the pool hall.

I want to apologize for not using my right name in this story. My dear mother, who is in heaven now, would never want to know her little boy was such a wicked kid. I got away with a lot with my mother. She thought I was such a good little boy because I never sassed her, did my chores and whenever asked to do something, I did it. That was my out. In later years, my mother would say, "What? You did this? You did what?"

25

BONES IN A BURNT BARN

by Shayla Clark

The fire siren cried in the small town of Newport early on the morning of August 4, 1936. At the call, firemen approached the hazardous scene: a pair of barns about five feet apart burning together. Locals and firefighters scrambled in the early morning to rescue what items of value they could before the spectacular blaze consumed the barns entirely.

Unsuccessful attempts to enter one of the barns led to the complete destruction of almost all of the contents of Cora Edwards's barn. Stored inside were three new "autos" and one truck owned by Newport neighbor Gordon Snyder. The autos, along with a number of farm implements and a quantity of household goods owned by Mrs. Edwards, were completely destroyed. At the time of the incident, the source of the fire could not be determined. According to later reports from fire officials, it was determined that the fire originated in the barn of Cora Edwards.

According to the same reports, the fire from the Edwards barn spread to the surrounding dry grass. Ultimately, the fire in the grass led to the combustion of the barn owned by Warren Fitch. On the receiving end of the blaze in the grass, some of the contents of the Fitch barn were rescued, including a tractor.

However, an even bigger spectacle was about to occur. Newport locals assumed that, following the fire, there was no work to be done besides the cleanup effort. That is, until Anna Weaver came to firefighters with an upsetting suspicion that her twenty-seven-year-old son, Albert Weaver, was in the Edwards barn at the time of the fire.

Albert Weaver was, like his mother, a member of one of the few Black families in Newport at the time. Albert "Al" Weaver spent the days of his young adulthood mainly working on nearby farms. In the habit of going off for days at a time to work on these farms, Al always returned home the following Saturday evening. Aside from farmwork, Al spent his time as an amateur boxer in the community.

Al had broken his routine of returning to his parents' residence on the Sunday before the fire happened. Anna Weaver was alarmed but initially did not act on her son's disappearance. The question of where Al was was only heightened when Anna decided to go to authorities, in accordance with remarks made by her husband, Charles.

Charles at the time was very ill. When Al did not return, Charles made "rambling remarks of a sick man." He had a strange intuition about Al's disappearance the day after the fire, stating that "he won't be home. He was bumped off last night in that barn that burned." This sent Anna to the firemen to request that the barn remains be searched for her son.

Initially, the firemen did not take Anna's concerns seriously. It was stated that if there was someone in the barn at the time of the fire, it would have been noticed. Anna, however, convinced them to look. On August 5, 1936, the same day Anna searched for answers, the remains of Albert Weaver were found inside the Edwards barn. A few days later, on August 13, Charles Weaver succumbed to his illness and died. Some news articles stated that Charles died of a heart attack at receiving the information that his grave intuition about his son had been correct.

The gruesome discovery was made by Ward Weakley of Newport. Among the ashes, he found bones, later identified as parts of a right leg bone, a collarbone, parts of several ribs and parts of the vertebrae. More important, the remains of a blue shirt and work pants were also discovered. It was through finding clothing among the bones that a positive identification of Albert Weaver could be made.

Coroner James W. Graves of Herkimer conducted an inquest on the day of the discovery. One of the chief witnesses at the inquest was Thomas Weaver, Al's identical twin brother. Thomas had stated that he had seen Albert at Mac's Restaurant in Newport on the night of August 3 and at about 12:15 a.m. on August 4. At this last sighting of Al, his brother noted that it seemed like Albert was heavily under the influence of liquor but that he was able to walk.

Before any significant time had passed, it was decided by Coroner Graves that Albert had come to his death from "shock and third-degree burns received while he was asleep on a bale of hay in the Edward's barn," specifically ruling that Albert's untimely death was purely accidental. Newport residents were never satisfied with the death being ruled an accident, because of Albert's notable fear of dark places. He was known to sing or whistle to bolster his courage when found in unlit areas.

Albert Weaver was not the only man initially missing in Newport. Arthur Mahardy had also not been seen around town in the days following the fire. Lacking the familial worry of his whereabouts, Mahardy was able to duck out of Newport with little attention. This did not mean, however, that Mahardy was not on people's radar in connection to the fire. He had previously been in trouble with the law, and Mahardy had been released from a stay in prison just two weeks before the night of the fire and the discovery of Albert Weaver's body.

At the suspicious circumstances of the fire, firemen called Sheriff Hoffman and Deputy Sheriff Hamblin. The sheriff and the deputy sheriff took descriptions from witnesses of a man in the vicinity at the time of the fire. Considering Mahardy's infractions with the law prior to the suspected barn burning, it was easy for the pair to conclude, based on the descriptions, that Arthur Mahardy was the man they were looking for.

At the time, Mahardy was by no means an outstanding citizen in the community. He had just been released from the Napanoch institution. On the rather ironic conclusion that Mahardy was determined to be "normal mentally," he served his time at Napanoch in connection with an earlier crime—breaking and entering the home of a Herkimer resident. This and a few stays at the Elmira Correctional Facility indicated that Mahardy was a trouble-ridden individual.

Mahardy's past put him in the position as the preliminary suspect for the burnings. Officials suspected that he would have attempted to make a getaway, and the search for Mahardy began. The opportunity for him to escape almost worked out in the end. That is, until a year to the day of the fire, when Arthur Mahardy was suddenly located on a road that led to Herkimer. Deputy Sheriff Hamblin caught Mahardy carrying a suitcase and formally placed him under arrest on August 4, 1937, bringing him to the Herkimer jail on an arson charge.

At first, Mahardy claimed innocence to the events in the early morning of August 4, 1936, stating that he had been in Syracuse at the time of the fire. Authorities were not satisfied. The fire, Al's death and Mahardy's yearlong

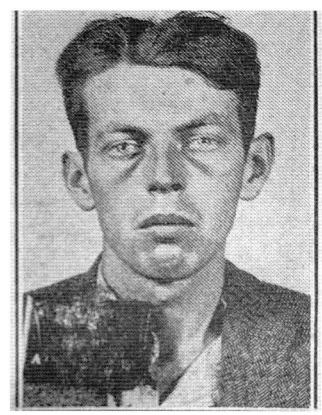

Arthur Mahardy. *Editors' collection.*

seeming disappearance from Newport were too "on point" to ignore. Through the diligent work of authorities, the ability to prove that Mahardy was in Newport on the night of the tragedy started a chain reaction to his confession. Arthur Mahardy had murdered Albert Weaver.

After three days of intense questioning, the confession from Mahardy was made to jailer Daniels on August 11, 1937.

Mahardy recalled what had led to the death of Albert Weaver, starting with his actions the day prior, on August 3, 1936. He stated that he had spent most of that morning at the Claude Hartman gasoline station. From there, he went to his home in Newport, where his grandmother resided. Mahardy chopped wood for most of the afternoon and had dinner. After that, he listened to the radio until about 8:00 p.m. and went to bed.

The early turn in to bed was short-lived. At about 10:00 p.m., Mahardy concluded that he could not sleep and found his way to a nearby street corner, where he met Albert Weaver. It is unsettling to think that, had Mahardy not gotten out of bed or gotten out of bed sooner or a little later, he perhaps might have never crossed paths with Albert Weaver, averting the tragedy that ended Albert's life.

Nonetheless, the two men became a pair and together went to Spellman's for a drink. Following this, they crossed the street to the hotel, where they got more drinks. As if the two prior locations did not quite satisfy their appetite for liquor, Mahardy and Weaver decided to walk down to Mac's restaurant and had something more to drink there. This is when Thomas, Albert's brother, saw him at the establishment owned by William McKinley Bateman.

Mahardy went on with his confession. "Weaver wanted to take a walk." The two walked to the bridge in Newport and stood there talking for what Mahardy accounted to be two hours. They then returned to Mac's, where they stayed until the proprietor closed the establishment. The pair found themselves back at the corner where their night had begun. At this point, Weaver "said he was going down to the hotel"—the Pioneer Inn—to see if he could "get another drink."

After a short time, Al returned to meet Mahardy at the corner. A pair once again, the two walked up toward the schoolhouse, then "toward Weaver's home." Mahardy claimed that it was Albert Weaver's idea to go into the Edwards barn to "sleep off their jag."

Mahardy's confession at this point turned from a tale of drunken endeavors to one of murder. Having entered the barn, an argument between the two men quickly ensued over the forthcoming boxing championship between Lou "The Hurricane" Ambers and the champion, Tony Canzoneri. On Mahardy's account, he and Weaver attempted to make a bet on the outcome, but both men wanted to bet on "The Hurricane," with a twenty-five-cent prize at stake. As a result of the controversy, Mahardy claimed he hit Weaver on the chin and then behind the ear while enraged. Weaver was struck down and "fell to the ground" over twenty-five cents.

Mahardy would later change his confession to jailer Daniels, stating that he struck Weaver with a weapon: a large rock in the toe of a sock. It is also worth noting that this weapon was suspected to be capable of crushing a man's skull. Furthermore, the weapon was found in the suitcase that Mahardy had at the time of his arrest. But Mahardy always stuck to his story that he struck Weaver down and set the fire to cover his tracks.

"I immediately saw that he was dead," Mahardy was reported to have said to Daniels during his confession. From there, Albert was dragged to the corner of the Edwards barn, where Mahardy "touched a match to a bunch of hay," which then became the source of the barn's fire. Concluding his confession, Mahardy recounted how he returned to his home in Newport to lie down for a while. And when the fire siren cried early on the morning of August 4, 1936, Mahardy took it upon himself to return to the scene of the crime he had just committed. One might also think that Mahardy went to watch Albert Weaver's fiery grave consume his body, seeing that the cover-up of the murder was done.

Mahardy's confession statement was taken and signed by him at the witness of Daniels and the night jailer, Martin Manion of Newport. The confession shocked the small town of Newport at its release. But for Mahardy, it was said he was "considerably relieved after telling his story."

From here, Mahardy was charged with first-degree murder. Furthermore, District Attorney Carl W. Peterson said that Mahardy's case would probably go before the December grand jury of 1937. Peterson was confident and spoke highly of the work done by officials to uncover the case.

On August 12, 1937, the *Rome Daily Sentinel* reported that an indictment of first-degree murder would be sought against Arthur Mahardy. Twenty-seven at the time, Mahardy was removed to the famous Gillette cell, where he joined the list of murderers kept there.

At the reaction to Mahardy's shocking confession, some skepticism arose. Many Newport residents agreed that certain parts of Mahardy's confession seemed to conflict. The point was continually made that the fact of Albert Weaver's presence in the barn needed explanation. Few conceded to the idea that Albert had gone to the barn on his own, again, out of his fear of the dark.

Mahardy's confession, though damning, included some deviation from the facts. Following investigation into the matter and the gathering of evidence against Mahardy, the drunken night he and Weaver shared was not exactly as he described it. In fact, for Mahardy, it wasn't drunken at all.

After a more factual investigation, it was reported by proprietors of the establishments that Mahardy had not, in fact, accompanied Weaver, as his confession claimed. "All recalled" seeing Weaver the night before his death but could not clearly recall Mahardy's company. Henry Kiefer of the Pioneer Inn denied that there was any truth to Mahardy's confession that he had served them drinks. No one could recall Mahardy ever taking more than one drink, and some could not recall him ever drinking.

Furthermore, in a more curious realization, the bartender at Mac's restaurant the night before the tragedy had a special connection to Arthur Mahardy. Frank Mahardy, the bartender at Mac's on the last day of Albert's life, was the father of Arthur Mahardy. Frank denied that his son had been in Mac's that night but confirmed that Albert Weaver had been.

December 16, 1937, rolled around, and Arthur Mahardy was scheduled to go before Herkimer County judge Frank Shall. Mahardy's indictment had changed from first- to second-degree murder, as there was considerable doubt as to whether Mahardy had killed Weaver with the blows to the head like he contested or if he had killed Weaver in setting the barn on fire. Exactly how Albert Weaver died could never be exactly determined.

Regardless of the actions that caused Albert's death, Mahardy knew he was to blame. Not wanting to go to trial, Mahardy pled guilty to the charges of second-degree murder. He had already requested his attorney, Judge Arnold Blumberg, to refrain from making any plea for mercy. In response to Arthur's guilty plea, District Attorney Carl W. Peterson waived his right to make a counterplea for that reason. A small gathering of people awaited

Mahardy as he walked into the huge courtroom. Judge Shall's remarks to Mahardy were brief but "kindly," as the Little Falls *Evening Times* put it.

"It is necessary to say here that I regret the necessity of this," Judge Shall said to Mahardy. "I want to believe that there is some mental twist that has caused you to commit this crime.…The law says that the sentence must be not less than 20 years in prison nor more than your natural life, and I do sentence you to that."

This was the judge's first instance of being called upon to sentence a confessed murderer. When it came time to walk out of the courtroom, Mahardy was left with a sentence to serve twenty years to life for his involvement in Albert Weaver's death. It is said that Mahardy accepted the sentence with no outward display of emotion, simply a quiver to his lip, perhaps the appropriate reaction of a guilty man acknowledging his crimes.

Arrangements were made for him to be moved to Attica, a short distance from Buffalo. Under the terms of his sentence, Mahardy had a chance at early freedom, with the possibility to obtain parole in just thirteen years of hard time and work while incarcerated in Attica.

Arthur Mahardy remained in Attica Prison until his death on February 5, 1964, at the age of fifty-two.

Exactly how Albert Weaver died will never truly be known. Some believed that Albert was not killed by Mahardy directly; rather, that the fire ended his life. Albert Weaver was laid to rest, like his father and the rest of his family at their respective times, in Newport Cemetery. Who knows? Had Albert Weaver not been killed, maybe he would have gone on to fight Lou "The Hurricane" Ambers for the championship. And, in a turn of events, maybe someone would have died over a twenty-five-cent bet for Albert Weaver to win.

26

BURGLARY AND FIRE IN EAST SCHUYLER

BY SUSAN R. PERKINS

The original Baum Homestead was built about 1820 on Steuben Road in East Schuyler. It was purchased by Henry Phillip Baum (1791–1858) from Laurence Rinkle (ca. 1778–1870) in 1826. Henry Phillip was married to Catherine (Barth) (1789–1846). They had seven children, one of whom was a son, Peter (1814–1877), who was left the homestead following his father's death.

Peter Baum married Elmira (1827–1917), who decided she wanted the 1820 house torn down and a new house built fashioned after an Italianate mansion in Natchez, Mississippi. Peter built the twenty-room mansion in 1863–64 at a cost of $10,000. An undated and unnamed newspaper clipping stated the following: "The solid walls were made by a man named Cornelius Kane, an Irishman. A carpenter named Borden designed the woodwork, carved it by hand at home, and assembled at home on the spacious lawns, a sort of forerunner to pre-fabrication." There was cathedral glass of ruby red in the main front entrance protected by a wrought-iron grille. The hall had gold background wallpaper. The mansion was furnished with oil paintings, vases and chairs purchased in Europe. There was a second parlor with the original lace curtains, fireplace, solid mahogany tables and stands, mirrors and statuettes. The mansion was filled with antiques. No wonder it drew the attention of would-be thieves.

The home stayed in the Baum family, with granddaughter Ruth Elmira Cramer (1892–1963) and her husband, Louis Sass (1892–1966), living there.

Emma Baum Cramer inside the Baum home in Schuyler. Emma (1868–1969) was the daughter of Peter and Elmira Baum and was married to Charles Cramer (1862–1905). Their daughter was Ruth Elmira Cramer (1892–1963). *Courtesy of Herkimer County Historical Society.*

The mansion had been vacant in 1965 after Ruth's death two years before, and Louis was living in Herkimer and only used it as a summer residence. On October 8, Beulah Johnson reported to the Schuyler volunteer firemen about 4:10 a.m. that the Baum mansion was on fire. It took twenty-five firemen and three fire trucks to fight the blaze. All that was left of the mansion was the foundation, chimney and a few antiques. Flames had reached a 1956 car that appeared to have become stuck in the mud. As a result, the gas tank exploded. It was discovered that there were costly antiques in the back of the car that had been badly burned and that the license plate had been removed.

The firemen were returning to the station when they spotted a man walking on Route 5 about six miles from the fire heading west toward Utica. The man's clothes were wet. The firemen telephoned East Herkimer State Police to report the suspicious man. They responded immediately and apprehended him. He was identified as Frank Cornell, age twenty-five, of 202 Congress Street in Troy, New York. He was charged with third-degree burglary.

When Cornell was questioned by state police, he said he was "the lookout" and that an unidentified Albany man had loaded Cornell's car with antiques. The *Utica Observer Dispatch* of Saturday, October 8, 1965, reported the following:

> *Cornell said he was walking down Route 5 about seven miles from Utica when he "hitched" a ride with an unidentified Schuyler fireman. The fireman told Cornell he had been fighting a fire all night but would take him to Utica. Cornell said he told the fireman that he wanted to get a bus for Buffalo. He inquired at the bus station as to what time the next bus left for Albany, not Buffalo. Cornell then went to the railroad station, but returned to the bus terminal where the firemen and State Police took him into custody for questioning.*
>
> *Cornell said his accomplice, after loading the car with antiques, tried to back the car out of the driveway, but it became stuck in the mud. He was afraid that the noise of the spinning wheels might attract attention, so he "took off."*

After Cornell's arrest, he was remanded to the Herkimer County Jail. It took until April 7, 1966, for Frank Cornell to be charged with third-degree burglary and second-degree grand larceny. I couldn't find if another person was involved or what happened to Frank after the charges were made.

27
KILLER GHOSTS

by Dennis Webster

Herkimer, NY: The killer ghosts walk the jail in the dead of the squid-ink night, past the pale moonbeams obscured by the rusted cell bars. Criminal phantasms looking for their next victim but being of another realm, they can no longer maim or kill those of our mortal plane. When a murder is committed, there is a spiritual soul stain that is smeared and leaves a sad mark upon our world. One place that houses the ghosts of a past tragic death is the 1834 Herkimer Jail. The gray block building nestled on Main Street in Herkimer, New York, had held three convicted murderers, all of whom had taken different paths to placement within the steel-barred jail cells. The ghosts of the convicted killers—Roxalana Druse, Chester Gillette and Jean Gianini—haunt the jail, and many volunteers, tourists and staff have had numerous encounters with them. Professional ghost hunters have recorded disembodied voices and cries from the afterlife, along with ectoplasm-forming entities. The investigators have also been touched and pushed. Paranormal instances from the killer ghosts include the smells of perfume and cologne and all manners of knocking, banging and footsteps. Learning of these killers, their crimes and their demises, you'll understand why their ghosts travel through an afterworld portal to haunt the place that caged them, restrained them and held them while their souls awaited their fates. Before, dear reader, you learn of the haunts, you must become familiar with the people behind the

1834 Herkimer County Jail. *Editors' collection.*

crimes and the details of the deaths they dealt before encountering their own sealed spectral fates.

Our first killer ghost who haunts the 1834 Herkimer County Jail is the ax-murdering Roxalana Druse (1847–1887). She was a battered and abused wife of the much older William Druse, who slashed at her with a horse whip for disobedience. On a cold December day in 1884, Roxalana had enough of being abused by her husband and shot him in the head with a revolver she had hidden in her apron. She then chopped off William's head with an ax. Roxalana then quartered William's body with the chopping device, then threw the bloody raw pieces into the stove and cooked them until they were flesh-charcoal pieces, smoke-stained bone fragments and residual bodily ashes. Roxalana dumped the remains of her husband into a nearby marsh, then took the ax and revolver, wrapped them in a blanket and threw them into a pond. William was reported missing by the police, and an investigation led to the discovery of his remains as well as the hidden ax and revolver. Roxalana was arrested and charged with murder. She languished in the 1834 Herkimer Jail; the trial was held across the street in the Herkimer County Courthouse. The trial lasted two weeks, and Roxalana was found guilty. She was hanged in the front yard of the jail. Her hanging involved her standing on a platform, a weight dropping and her body being yanked off into the air. This was in stark contrast to the method of hanging that involved the body dropping through a platform. Roxalana suffered and took time to die; she was strangled and didn't die instantly. The hanging was so gruesome that she would be the last woman hanged in New York State. The electric chair was introduced for capital punishment. The jail has been investigated by ghost hunters. They have recorded a woman's cries in the area where Roxalana had been housed. There's a sadness in her spirit that hovers in the place where an abused woman paid with her life for her ax-wielding strikes. Her ghost wanders the jail and says that she'll respond to those who exhibit kindness and sympathy to her plight. Being bound for all eternity to the 1834 Herkimer Jail is her eternal punishment.

The second killer ghost who haunts the 1834 Herkimer County Jail is the womanizing skull-basher, Chester Gillette (1883–1908). This handsome killer fried to death in the electric chair in Auburn, New York, for the murder of his pregnant girlfriend, Grace Brown. Chester was a handsome and ambitious young man who came from a poor family who gave their lives to the service of the Salvation Army. Chester was described as charming, and he attracted a multitude of young ladies, who swooned at the dark-haired bachelor. He went to work for his rich uncle at his skirt factory in Cortland, New York. Chester didn't take long to place his eager eye upon the lovely farmer's daughter, Grace Brown. She was one of the sewers in the factory, and as fate would have it, Grace had her opal ring slip off her finger, whereupon Chester swooped it up and placed it back on her finger.

Roxalana Druse. *Editors' collection.*

He won Grace's heart and swept her off her feet, until he became bored and started seeking other ladies in the factory and spending his free time playing tennis and commiserating with the upper-crust socialites of Cortland. He had no time for a lovesick, factory-working farmer's daughter. But Grace revealed that she was pregnant. Chester arranged a date with murder, but Grace thought they were eloping. He carried his suitcase and beloved tennis racket. He took her into the Adirondacks, where they checked into Glenmore Inn on Big Moose Lake. Chester signed in under an assumed name. He took Grace out on the lake for a relaxing rowboat trip. He then took out his tennis racket and struck Grace in the head with an overhead blow, then threw her body into the dark,

Grace Brown and Chester Gillette. *Editors' collection.*

cold waters. Chester fled the scene, but he was eventually caught. His cell at the 1834 jail was adorned with hundreds of photos of young, attractive ladies he had cut out from magazines. Many lady admirers were entranced by and romantically interested in the handsome killer and wrote him, visited him in jail and packed the courthouse during his murder trial. It became a media sensation. The two-week trial concluded with the jury taking just two hours to declare him guilty and sentence him to death in the electric chair. Chester was executed on March 30, 1908, with his fleshy, earthbound husk charred by the deathly voltage. But his ghost remained on our plane and visits his jail cell on a regular basis. Many visitors to the 1834 Herkimer Jail, especially young ladies, say that they have seen and felt Chester's ghost. When a team of ghost hunters investigated the jail, they had on their team a beautiful, young redheaded girl of nineteen. She felt her shoulders being touched and her hair stroked. Even in the afterlife, Chester is drawn to the mortal bodies of cute living ladies. Just beware that if you are a lovely lady and you visit his cell at the 1834 Herkimer Jail, Chester's ghost just might get up close and personal.

Our third killer ghost who haunts the 1834 Herkimer County Jail is the schoolteacher murderer, Jean Gianini (1898–1988). He was only sixteen years old when he killed his teacher, Lida Beecher, in Poland, New York, on March 27, 1914. Unlike our previous killer ghosts, Jean was determined to be a young man of limited mental abilities. He had been deemed a "high-grade imbecile" by world-renowned alienist Dr. Henry Goddard, who had seen over forty thousand "imbeciles" in his esteemed career. Jean's murder trial was the lengthiest and costliest in the history of Herkimer County. He had been turned in to his father by his teacher for misbehavior and swore to get revenge on the beautiful young Miss Beecher, who was only twenty years old at the time of her death. Jean lured his teacher up Buck Hill Road in Poland, New York, then hit her in the head with a monkey wrench. He finished off her life with several stabs from a large knife he had borrowed from his father's kitchen. Jean returned the knife to the drawer, slept in his bed, then wandered the area's railroad tracks the next day until he was picked up by the sheriff. Jean quickly confessed, as his mental disability inhibited the feeling of empathy for what he had done. Jean was found not guilty by reason of insanity and spent almost the entirety of the rest of his life in an asylum for the criminally insane. He died at peace in a nursing home, but his spirit has been seen visiting his former cell and wandering the place where his life had hung in the balance. A date with the electric chair was avoided by a sympathetic jury. Ghost hunters have claimed that there's a spirit of a man who likes to play pranks and tug on the hair of the living, much like Jean had done as a schoolboy prankster.

So now you know that you can visit one historic and haunted place and experience the presence of Roxalana, Chester and Jean. Their souls reside forever trapped within the concrete walls and rusted steel bars. Just beware that playing with the souls of the dead can carry dangerous consequences. One can be haunted by killer ghosts of murdered past.

Dennis Webster is the published author of books on asylums, true crime and haunted locations. He's a ghost hunter with the Fort Schuyler Paranormal Society and has ghost hunted the 1834 Herkimer Jail, where he had interaction with the spirits of the criminally dead.

NOTES

6. The Troubled Life of Alton Vincent

1. 1880 United States Census; *Little Falls (NY) Evening Times*, November 26, 1962.
2. *Little Falls Evening Times*, October 19, 1892.
3. *Little Falls (NY) Journal and Courier*, June 4, 1895.
4. Ibid., September 4, 1895.
5. *Little Falls Evening Times*, November 15, 1895.
6. *Utica (NY) Daily Press*, July 30, 1900.
7. Ibid., July 30, 1900.
8. *Rome (NY) Sentinel*, April 15, 1901.
9. *Herkimer (NY) Evening Telegram*, September 31, 1914.
10. *Watertown (NY) Daily Times*, March 11, 1903.
11. *Richfield Springs (NY) Mercury*, July 16, 1903.
12. *Watertown Daily Times*, August 4, 1903.
13. *Watertown (NY) Re-Union*, December 12, 1903.
14. *Gloversville (NY) Daily Leader*, December 4, 1903.
15. *Utica (NY) Herald Dispatch*, August 6, 1908.
16. *Broadalbin (NY) Herald*, August 6, 1908.
17. *Syracuse (NY) Herald*, August 4, 1908.
18. *Ilion (NY) Citizen*, September 10, 1908.
19. *Utica Daily Press*, September 17, 1908.
20. Auburn Prison Records, New York State Archives.

NOTES

21. *Utica (NY) Sunday Tribune*, November 12, 1911.
22. *Little Falls Evening Times*, November 26, 1962.

17. He Shot Her in the Corset

23. "Deed of a Fiend," *Utica Saturday Globe*, April 10, 1915.
24. Nancy Helmer Folts, diary entry, April 6, 1915.
25. "Deed of a Fiend."
26. Ibid.
27. Ibid.
28. "Deed of a Fiend" and Nancy Helmer Folts's diary entry.
29. *Fort Plain (NY) Standard*, July 8, 1915; *Knickerbocker [News]* (Albany, NY), June 23, 1915. Photocopies courtesy of the Herkimer County Historical Society.

21. The Gillette Cell

30. *Ilion Citizen*, July 22, 1911.
31. *Knickerbocker Press* (Albany, NY), June 15, 1914; *Syracuse Daily Journal*, May 19, 1914.
32. Page 153, Law Notes, Vol. XIX, April 1915 to March 1916, Edward Thompson Company, Law Publisher, Northport, Long Island, New York, 1916.
33. *Utica Daily Press*, May 29, 1914.
34. *Waterville Times*, May 29, 1914.
35. Donna Rubin, "A Wolf in Sheep's Clothing," in Caryl Hopson and Susan R. Perkins, eds., *Murder & Mayhem in Herkimer County* (Charleston, SC: The History Press, 2019).
36. *Watertown Daily Standard*, June 29, 1924.
37. Ibid.
38. Ibid., July 10, 1924.
39. Caryl Hopson and Susan R. Perkins, "Wagner-Hotaling Murder of Little Falls," in Hopson and Perkins, eds., *Murder & Mayhem in Herkimer County*.
40. Ibid.
41. *Syracuse (NY) Journal*, December 29, 1927; January 23, 1928.
42. *Amsterdam (NY) Evening Recorder*, November 25, 1930.

Notes

43. *Ogdensburg (NY) Journal*, February 19, 1935; *Utica Daily Press*, January 23, 1931.
44. *Morning Herald* (Gloversville and Johnstown, NY), March 19, 1932.
45. *Troy (NY) Times*, January 23, 1932.
46. *Rome (NY) Sentinel*, March 21, 1932.
47. *Morning Herald*, April 5, 1932.
48. *St. Johnsville (NY) Enterprise and News*, July 10, 1935.
49. *Herkimer Evening Telegram*, May 24, 1968.

BIBLIOGRAPHY

1. Grave Behavior

Dieffenbacher, Jane. *This Green and Pleasant Land—Fairfield, New York*. 2nd ed. New York: Steffen Publishing, 2003, 227–30.
Fairfield Collection. Jas. B. Dungan to N.W. Folwell, December 9, 1833. Herkimer County Historical Society, FF1977.916.
———. "Records of the Proceedings of the College of Physicians and Surgeons of the Western District" (transcription). Herkimer County Historical Society, Herkimer, New York, 46.
Ilion (NY) Citizen. "Early Recollections." March, 20, 1903, 2.
New York State Legislature. "An Act for the Further Support of the College of Physicians and Surgeons of the Western District." Laws of the State of New York, March 30, 1820.
Norway (NY) Tidings 2, no. 10, October 1888.
O'Donnell, C.O. *Tip of the Hill: An Informal History of the Fairfield Academy and Medical College*. Boonville, NY: Black River Books, 1953, 112–13.
Tippetts, W.H. *Herkimer County Murders*. Herkimer, NY: H.P. Witherstine and Co., 1885, 6–8.

2. The Body Snatching of Harry Burrell

Herkimer County (NY) Journal.
Herkimer County (NY) News.

Bibliography

Herkimer (NY) Democrat.
Little Falls Historical Society archives. Little Falls, New York.
Utica (NY) Morning Herald.

3. Blond of Thirty Summers

Albany (NY) Argus. February 22, 1889.
Ancestry.com. Census, death and marriage notices. Civil War records. www.ancestry.com.
Evening Times (Little Falls, NY). October 8, 1879.
Fulton History. www.fultonhistory.com.

4. Oliver Curtis Perry

Auburn (NY) Bulletin. "Robber Perry's Story." February 21, 1992.
Casey, D., and D. Larkin. "From Dunmore to Middle Sprite: Irish Rural Settlement in New York." *Clogher Historical Society* 12, no. 2 (1986): 181–91.
Daily Times (Troy, NY). "Oliver Curtis Perry." March 1, 1892.
———. "The Train Robber's Story." April 29, 1895, 6.
Elmira (NY) Telegram. "Attacked a Keeper." April 14, 1895.
———. "Cruel, Cool Crook." February 28, 1892.
Fairport (NY) Herald. "Refuses All Clothing in Prison." April 19, 1913.
Herkimer (NY) Citizen. "Desperate Perry." February 23, 1892.
———. "We Don't Want Perry." March 1, 1892.
Holder, A., and F. Sweeney. *Our Songs: Americkana Arkana.* The Magic City. Accessed April 2018. www.themagiccitytrio.com.
Journal and Courier (Little Falls, NY). "Frankfort." June 17, 1896.
McDermott, M. "Outlaw Oliver Curtis Perry Leads Police on a Train Chase in Wayne County." *Democrat & Chronicle* (Rochester, NY). February 22, 2014.
Paine, J. "Two More Escaped Convicts Caught." Cortland Contrarian. Accessed February 28, 2018. www.jeffpainblogspot.com.
Spargo, T. *Wanted Man: The Forgotten Story of Oliver Curtis Perry, an American Outlaw.* New York: Bloomsbury, 2014.
Utica (NY) Daily Press. "Elk's Clam Bake." June 1899.
———. "Tracking the Fugitive." October 4, 1891.
Utica (NY) Morning Herald. "The Train Robber." February 21, 1892.
Utica (NY) Tribune. "Why Perry Is Not Tried." March 15, 1892.

Bibliography

5. No Minor Offense

Evening Times (Little Falls, NY). May 26, 1893.
Johnstown (NY) Daily Republican. "Bertha Valentine Testimony Libel." December 12, 1895.
Little Falls (NY) Journal and Courier. "Cramer Not Guilty." December 31, 1895.
Utica (NY) Daily Union. "Nellie Van Ever Testimony Rape." December 27, 1895.
———. "Witnesses and Summations." December 28, 1895.

7. The Backlash of Infidelity

Canajoharie (NY) Courier. "Brambach Factory Moves." May 1901.
Fulton County (NY) Republican. "Mangold Letter to Wife and Elope." April 14, 1904.
Gloversville (NY) Daily Leader. "Mangold Warrant & Support, Brambach Arrest." April 19, 1901.
New York Evening World. "Mangold Effigy." April 19, 1901.
New York Press. "Jury Upholds Horsewhipping." April 26, 1901.
New York Sun. "Horsewhipping Incident." April 19, 1901.

8. The Church Lady and the Forest Ranger

Albany (NY) Argus. "Game Protector Klock Convicted." February 14, 1908.
Herkimer (NY) Citizen. "Game Protector Klock Has Skipped the Country with a Young Girl." August 15, 1905.
———. "Ready to Face Charges." November 7, 1905.
Herkimer (NY) Evening Telegram. Fairfield Methodist Church meeting notices and appointment of trustees, their service guild and W.C.T.S. on many dates, including May 9, 1945, March 4, 1946, March 18, 1947, March 26, 1947, February 22, 1950, May 18, 1957, and September 30, 1955.
New York Evening Post. "Long Chase of Timber Looters." October 5, 1907.
Otsego (NY) Farmer. "In Central New York." August 18, 1905.
PDX History. "The Lewis and Clark Centennial." Portland, Oregon. http://www.pdxhistory.com.
Richfield Springs (NY) Mercury. "Clippings from Exchanges." March 1, 1906.
Utica (NY) Daily Press. "Miss Barnes' Whereabouts Known." August 30, 1905.

Utica (NY) Herald Dispatch. "Klock Returns Home to Vote." November 7, 1905.
———. "Returns to Her Own Fireside." October 26, 1905.

9. Fanny, the Female Firebug

Ilion Citizen. "They Confess Arson." February 22, 1906.
Rome (NY) Daily Sentinel. "Two Women Free." April 11, 1906.
Syracuse (NY) Post Standard. "Supreme Court at Herkimer." April 10, 1906.
Utica (NY) Herald Dispatch. "Stolen Property Was Recovered." February 20, 1906.
Utica (NY) Journal. "Woman Firebug Tells of Her Daring Deed." February 25, 1906.

10. The Houdini of Horse Thieves

Amsterdam (NY) Evening Recorder. "Around the City." December 8, 1908.
Fulton County (NY) Republican. "Gypsy Mike Stung Them." May 21, 1908.
Ilion (NY) Citizen. "Brought Back to the Fold." September 17, 1908.
Rome (NY) Daily Sentinel. "Adventures of Gypsy Mike." May 13, 1908.
Utica (NY) Herald Dispatch. "Horses Recovered." May 4, 1908.
———. "Moss Island Fire…" September 18, 1908.
———. "Six Persons Escaped from Herkimer Jail." September 7, 1908.
———. "Young Man Had a Close Call." September 19, 1908.
Waterville (NY) Times. "Escaped from Herkimer Jail." September 8, 1908.

11. When Yeggs Hit Herkimer County

Herkimer (NY) Democrat. January 14, 1880; October 23, 1895.
Ithaca (NY) Daily Journal. January 20, 1910.
Marion (NY) Enterprise. January 28, 1910.
Ogdensburg (NY) Journal. January 21, 1910.
Outlook Magazine. "John the Yeggman." 98 (May–August 1911).
Scientific American. "The Ungentle Art of Burglary." January 27, 1906.

BIBLIOGRAPHY

12. The Textile Strike Riot

Little Falls (NY) Journal and Courier. October 22. 1912.
New York Call (New York, NY). October 31, 1912; October 21, 1912; October 22, 1912; October 25, 1912; November 19, 1912.
Rome (NY) Daily Sentinel. October 18, 1912.
Schenectady (NY) Gazette. December 31, 1912; October 23, 1912.
Snyder, Robert E. "Women, Wobblies, and Workers' Rights: The 1912 Textile Strike in Little Falls, New York." *New York History* 60, no. 1 (January 1978).
State Department of Labor. "The Little Falls Textile Workers' Dispute." Albany, New York, 1913.
State Factory Investigating Commission. "Hearing of the State Factory Investigating Commission Held at the Plant of the Dingman Company Little Falls, New York, August 12, 1912." 2nd Report. Volumes 2 and 3.
Syracuse (NY) Herald. Saturday Evening. October 26, 1912.
Syracuse (NY) Journal. Friday, October 18, 1912.
Utica (NY) Herald Dispatch. October 14. 1912; October 25, 1912; October 29, 1912; October 30, 1912; December 31, 1912; November 7, 1912.
Van Horne, Schuyler. "The Little Falls Textile Strike of 1912." Unpublished independent study. Hobart College. 1968.

13. The Case of the Rat-Fink Roommate

Genealogy Trails History Group. News Stories of Clarence Kelley murder from *Daily News* (Batavia, NY), collected by Nan Starjak. http://genealogytrails.com/ny/herkimer/news_kelleymurder.html.
Rome Daily Sentinel. "Kelly Murder Clue." April 27, 1921.
Utica (NY) Herald Dispatch. "Almon Cole Is Held on Technical Charge." April 27, 1921.
Utica (NY) Morning Telegram. "Young Man Brought to Herkimer in Connection with Kelly Case." April 28, 1921.
Watertown City Directory. "George Wallace." 1922. Ancestry.com. U.S. City Directories, 1822–1995. Provo, UT: Ancestry.com Operations Inc., 2011.

BIBLIOGRAPHY

14. Organized Crime in Herkimer County

Editors of Encyclopaedia Britannica. "Black Hand." December 20, 2017. Accessed July 31, 2020. www.britannica.com.

Herkimer County Historical Society and the Herkimer County Records Department.

History.com. "Origins of the Mafia." October 29, 2009. Accessed July 31, 2020. www.history.com.

Ilion Citizen. December 12, 1907.

15. Grace under Pressure

Evening Times (Little Falls, NY). "Newport Child Released from Jail." August 4, 1920.

Familysearch.org. 1920 United States Federal Census. Frankfort, Herkimer, New York; Roll: T625_1115. Page: 3A; Enumeration District: 41.

———. 1940 United States Federal Census. Frankfort, Herkimer, New York; Roll: m-t0627-02543; Page: 61B; Enumeration District: 22–59.

Findagrave.com. Memorial page for Grace E. Haley Parks (1903–1979), Find a Grave Memorial no. 13659351. Accessed March 19, 2021.

Herkimer (NY) Evening Telegram. "Newport Notes." August 13, 1959.

"Juvenile Detention in New York: Then and Now." Display at John Jay College of Criminal Justice by the city Department of Juvenile Justice. http://www.correctionhistory.org/html/chronicl/djj/djj20yrs3.htm#TopDJJ.

16. Wild, Wild Beaver River

Albany Knickerbocker Press. "Accuse Lumberjack of Shooting Up Town." October 2, 1923. John Trimble was identified as the shooter at Beaver River Station. He was arrested on a first-degree assault charge and locked up in the jail at Herkimer County in lieu of not being able to post a $500 bond. In Bill Marleau's book *Big Moose Station* (1986, p. 215), he included an unidentified source for a comprehensive article called "World War One Vet Runs Amuck with Gun," with the date of October 8, 1924. But I have several other sources that note this event took place in October 1923. "Tennessee" John I. Trimble was arrested by Troopers McCredie and Gilson at his camp and arraigned before Justice Charles Wright in Old

Bibliography

Forge before being taken to jail in Herkimer. According to the 1925 New York State Census for Beaver River, Maude Lang was the proprietor of a boardinghouse and the mother of four Lang children. William Brown was a boarder but was listed as her husband in the 1924 shooting articles. She appears to have married Brown by 1930 and had at least one child with him, according to the Altamont, New York census in 1930.

Donnelly. William B. "A Short History of Beaver River." Beaver River, NY: Property Owners Association, 1979. Donnelly notes that Beaver River was sold by Dr. William Seward Webb in 1899 to a mill operator, Firman Ouderkirk, who then sold it to Bert B. Bullock. After the Norridgewock burned in 1914, Bullock began selling off lots east and west of the hotel property from 1915 to 1917. References to land deeds at Beaver River still refer to the Bert Bullock Block.

Hudson River–Black River Regulating District Bulletin. "Black River Regulating District Turns 100." Article posted by Megan for HRBRRD, August 13, 2019. www.hrbrrd.com/news-bulletins.

Lowville (NY) Journal and Republican. "Board Will Clear Land." August 9, 1923. The BRRD Board received only one bid of $986,000 for the removal of the timber and the stumps above the Stillwater dam. They determined they could do it themselves for much less money without removing the stumps, which were cut to twelve inches below the anticipated water levels in the flooded lands. On the construction site of the dam, there are about sixty men employed by Scott Brothers, while at other points on the reservoir, the St. Regis Paper Company has about two hundred men busy lumbering pulp wood that they are buying, while the regulating board has about four hundred men clearing the land to be flooded and burning brush.

———. "In Typical Cow Boy Style." March 20, 1924. Mary's fiancé was Harry James Smith—ironically, with the same name as Jess Eilliot-Smith's husband. They obtained a license and were married in Old Forge the following day.

———. "3,960 Acres to Be Flooded at Once." June 7, 1923. The Williams Bill, amending the state's conservation laws, allowed the conservation commissioner to award contracts written by the Black River Regulating District for the removal of timber of state lands.

———. "Two Lose Lives in Burning of Vincent's Hotel at Beaver River." May 15, 1924. The fire was discovered at 4:00 a.m. on the morning of May 12, by a workman at the station. The *Richfield Springs Mercury* of May 29, 1924, noted the housekeeper's name as Mrs. Amos Des Champo.

Bibliography

George Vincent was fifty-five years old and had purchased this hotel from Monroe Bullock, father of Bert B. Bullock, in 1923.

Malone Telegram. "Death Toll in Fire Uncertain." May 13, 1924. Comprehensive article describing how state troopers were summoned to examine the ruins for other victims. According to an article on the fire, about six hundred men were in the camps, and they came from Canada, Russia, Germany, Italy and all over the United States.

Marleau, Bill. *Big Moose Station*. N.p.: Marleau Family Press, 1986. Marleau reprints a news article titled "Utica Paper" of October 8, 1924, about the arrest of Charles Ellerby and Harry Smith. However, this date is incorrect. The *Utica Observer Dispatch* of October 1923 published a detailed article on the raid by the Prohibition officers. The *Watertown Daily Standard* of December 7, 1923, reported that Harry Smith of Beaver River pled not guilty to possession of one drink of whisky, $1,000 bail set by Judge Cooper in Utica court (page 215).

———. Bill Marleau and his brother were two of the kids who helped Ellerby with his home-brew operation, which he conducted at Dave DesJardin's Summit Hotel in Big Moose (page 217).

Thompson, Pat. *Beaver River—Oasis in the Wilderness*. Beaver River, NY: Beaver River Press, 2000, 145.

Utica (NY) Daily Dispatch. "Begin Drying Out Beaver River." June 20, 1924. The cans were brought in by Harry Lang from Tupper Lake, and he was promptly arrested.

Utica (NY) Daily Press. June 16, 1899. Classified ad for B.B. Bullock's Norridgewock House at Beaver River in the summer of 1899. Accommodations at seven to ten dollars a week. The ad was listed throughout May and June 1899 in the Utica papers.

Watertown (NY) Daily Times. "Beaver River Stabbing Fatal." May 8, 1924. The Polish lumberjack reportedly died from injuries sustained during the lumber camp brawl.

———. "Says Troopers Exceed Rights." August 14, 1924.

18. Don't Ask Any Questions

Ancestry.com. Census, marriage and divorces.

New York State Marriage Index. "Clara M. Lawson." July 15, 1920.

Utica (NY) Herald Dispatch. December 28, 1906 (marriage of Leigh J. Perkins to Gertie Kibbie); July 15, 1920 (marriage of Leigh J. Perkins to Clara M. Lawson).

BIBLIOGRAPHY

19. The Murder of Winifred Getman

Ancestry.com. www.ancestry.com.
Citizen Advertiser (Auburn, NY). December 21, 1933.
Fulton History. www.fultonhistory.com.
Glimmerglass (Cooperstown, NY). July 12, 1922.
Herkimer (NY) Evening Telegram. May 20, 1958.
Utica (NY) Herald Dispatch. July 16, 1916; October 6, 1916.
Utica (NY) Observer Dispatch. July 4, 1922.

20. Trial to Triumph: An Immigrant Family's Story

Albany (NY) Knickerbocker News. June 1, 1959.
Ancestry.com.
Fulton History. www.fultonhistory.com.
Herkimer Evening Telegram. September 26, 1952; October 1, 1952; November 21, 1952.
Leader Herald (Johnstown, NY). August 16, 1955; January 26, 1961; November 6, 1962; May 13, 1963; January 3, 1970.
Morning Herald (Gloversville and Johnstown, NY). May 7, 1954.
Schenectady (NY) Gazette. May 29, 1959 (picture of Sylvia Lavista as bride).
Utica (NY) Daily Press. January 14, 1974.
Utica (NY) Observer Dispatch. January 12, 1935 (picture of Mrs. Rocco Lavista wedding).

22. Criminal Melodrama

Ancestry.com. 1905 New York State Census; 1910 Federal Census; Massachusetts Marriage Index, 1901–1955; Michigan Marriage Records, 1867–1952; New York State, Sing Sing Prison Admission Registers, 1865–1938; New York, County Marriages, 1907–1936; World War I Draft Registration, 1917–1918, Missouri.
Buffalo (NY) Commercial. "Mulford's Fate Went to the Jury This Afternoon." January 5, 1921.
Buffalo (NY) Courier. "Case of 'Whitey' Slover Accused of Yellen Slaying Will Go to Jury." January 14, 1921.
———. "Gunmen Shot Proprietor of Second Hand Store: Not Expected to Live; Arrest." November 26, 1920.

Bibliography

———. "Hold Woman Three Men in Yellen Murder Case." November 28, 1920.
———. "Lillian Gusse Granted Freedom by Court and Husband's Pardon." March 3, 1921.
———. "Mulford Murder Trial." January 5, 1921.
———. "Notices of Appeal Stays Execution." February 10, 1921.
———. "Resort to Secret Plan to Arraign Yellen Suspects." December 7, 1920.
———. "Slover Slayer of Yellen Says State's Witness." January 8, 1921.
———. "Woman Tells of Daring Crimes." November 27, 1920.
Buffalo (NY) Courier Express. "Lieut. Condren Dies; Hero of Daring Arrest Dies." March 13, 1943.
Buffalo (NY) Enquirer. "Attack Men in Courtroom, Yellen Boys Leap on Gang Accused of Death of Abram Yellen, Father." November 27, 1920.
———. "Buffalo Murderers to Die Tomorrow Night, All Ready: Both Abandon Hope of Stay." January 11, 1922.
———. "Death Sentence Imposed on Two; Prison for Webber." January 21, 1921.
———. "Hartford Women Not One Involved in Poison Case; Was Oneida Girl?" January 9, 1921.
———. "Last Words of Mulford and Slover: Condemned Men Talk to Enquirer Reporter at Sing Sing Prison." January 24, 1921.
Buffalo (NY) Evening News. "Clothier Shot, Life in Danger." November 26, 1920.
———. "Mulford Balks on Telling of Yellen Murder," January 5, 1921.
———. "Wife's Story Is Repudiated by Mulford." January 7, 1921.
Hartford (CT) Courant. "Come and Bring Our Little Baby." January 11, 1921.
———. "Wife Declares Mulford Overjoyed to See Child." February 18, 1921.
Herkimer (NY) Evening Telegram. "Appeal to Governor to Save the Life of a Former Herkimer Boy." December 12, 1921.
———. "Mulford Pronounced Sane." December 15, 1921.
Herkimer Morning Herald. "Night Chef Missing also Fifty Dollars." October 5, 1914.
Joyce, Rob. Research collection on Raymond Mulford.
McCarthy, Raymond. "Slayers of Abraham Yellen and Jeweler Weitz Put to Death." *Buffalo (NY) Inquirer*, January 13, 1922.
McLaughlin, Vance. "638 Homicides Occurring in Buffalo, 1902–1936." Homicide Research. 2013, 41–42. www.homicideresearch.com.
New York Evening World. "Webber Pleads Guilty." January 19, 1921.

New York State Archives. Albany, New York. Auburn Prison, Registers of Male Inmates Discharged, 1918–1943.

———. Elmira Reformatory Biographical Registers and Receiving Plotters. Series Number B0141.

Norwich (NY) Bulletin. "Finding Missing Husband Is on Trial for Murder." January 7, 1921.

Rome (NY) Daily Sentinel. "Oneida Poisoning Figures in Murder Trial at Buffalo." January 7, 1921.

Syracuse (NY) Herald. "Jury in Murder Cases out Only 50 Minutes." January 6, 1921.

Utica (NY) Daily Press. "Raymond Mulford Indicted." January 20, 1915.

Utica (NY) Herald Dispatch. "Ray and Claude Mulford Sentenced." June 1906.

Utica (NY) Morning Telegram. "Women Blamed by Slayer for His Downfall." January 8, 1921.

23. Shootout at Camp Utica in Old Forge

Ancestry.com. www.ancestry.com.
Evening Tribune Times (Hornell, NY). February 8, 1927.
Fulton History. www.fultonhistory.com.
Herkimer (NY) Evening Telegram. December 21, 1927.
Journal and Republican & Lowville Times (Lowville, NY). February 16, 1927.
New York Sun. December 16, 1927; February 10, 1927; May 16, 1927.
Rome (NY) Daily Sentinel. February 9, 1927.
Utica (NY) Daily Press. February 10, 1927.

25. Bones in a Burnt Barn

Evening Times (Little Falls, NY). August 4, 1936; August 10, 1936; August 13, 1936; August 11, 1937; August 12, 1937; December 16, 1937.
Find a Grave. "Census Report of 1930." www.findagrave.com.
Fulton History. www.fultonhistory.com.
Rome (NY) Daily Sentinel. August 12, 1937.
Utica (NY) Daily Press. February 26, 1936.
Utica (NY) Observer Dispatch. August 12, 1937; December 16, 1937.

Bibliography

26. Burglary and Fire in East Schuyler

Ancestry. www.ancestry.com.
Find a Grave. www.findagrave.com.
Fulton History. www.fultonhistory.com.
Herkimer (NY) Evening Telegram. October 8, 1965; October 9, 1965; February 10, 1966; February 23, 1966; April 7, 1966.

Opposite: Old postcard of the 1834 Herkimer County Jail.

ABOUT FRIENDS OF HISTORIC HERKIMER COUNTY

Friends of Historic Herkimer County was established in 2004 as a 501(c)(3) not-for-profit organization with a mission to preserve and protect historic structures in Herkimer County, with a focus on the Historic 1834 Jail, in order to preserve the concept of the "Historic Herkimer Four Corners."

The Historic 1834 Jail is an anchor of the historic Four Corners area in the village's downtown, and it serves as a unique representative of Federal-style architecture as well as a colorful history as the county's long-standing jail facility up to the 1970s, with many notable inmates having the "privilege" of staying there.

The Four Corners attracts thousands of tourists, schoolchildren and researchers to its four distinctive historic structures. It serves to contribute to the revitalization of the Village of Herkimer's Business District and builds on the region's tourism industry.

About Friends of Historic Herkimer County

Help us open the doors of the jail for tours once again.

The Friends group has been working diligently to undertake major rehabilitation projects since 2004 to bring it back into a condition where public tours will be available. With the support of state and community grants, corporate and individual donations and fundraisers, we are close to our goal. You can help us get there by sending in a membership contribution.

For a five-dollar donation, you can become an Individual member.

For a ten-dollar donation, you can become a Family member.

For a fifteen-dollar donation, you can become a Business supporter.

Your additional contribution, if you are able to provide it, will help us even further to save the 1834 Jail. Please mail your membership donation to: Friends of Historic Herkimer County, PO Box 703, Herkimer, NY 13350.

For your support, you will receive a newsletter filled with updates on our renovation projects, interesting stories of the 1834 Jail and first invitations to jail events.

ABOUT THE EDITORS

Caryl Hopson and Susan Perkins have collaborated on previous books, including the Images of America series volumes of *Herkimer Village* (2008), *German Flatts* (2010), *Little Falls* (2010) and *Frankfort* (2013), and were co-editors of *Murder & Mayhem in Herkimer County* (2019). They shared a rewarding partnership in their years at the Herkimer County Historical Society, promoting and preserving the area's rich history. Susan Perkins served as the organization's registrar, administrative assistant and, finally, executive director for the last twenty-four of her thirty-eight years with the society. Caryl Hopson first came on board to type the new history of Herkimer County book in 1991 and stayed for a career of thirty years as the organization's secretary and administrative assistant. They both serve as board members of Friends of Historic Herkimer County.

Visit us at
www.historypress.com